Black
Crusaders
for Freedom

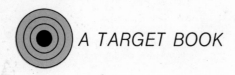A TARGET BOOK

Black Crusaders for Freedom

Edited, with commentary by Bennett Wayne

GARRARD PUBLISHING COMPANY
CHAMPAIGN, ILLINOIS

Picture credits:

Bettmann Archive: pp. 6, 13, 27, 54 (top), 77, 86, 127, 133, 164 (top)
Brown Brothers: pp. 57, 117, 124, 136, 147, 156 (top), 162
Culver Pictures: pp. 90, 104, 156 (bottom), 164 (bottom)
Detroit Public Library, Burton Historical Collection: p. 82
Library of Congress: pp. 44–45, 93
Michigan Historical Collections of the University of Michigan:
    p. 54 (bottom)
New York Public Library, Picture Collection: p. 62
New York Public Library, Schomburg Center for Research in
    Black Culture. Astor, Lenox, and Tilden
    Foundations: pp. 37, 73
Smith College Library, Sophia Smith Collection: p. 9

Library of Congress Cataloging in Publication Data

Wayne, Bennett, comp.
    Black crusaders for freedom.

    (Target)
    SUMMARY: Biographies of four Negroes famed for their
efforts in improving conditions for their race: Sojourner
Truth, Frederick Douglass, Harriet Tubman, and Booker
T. Washington.

    1. Negroes—Biography—Juvenile literature.
[1. Negroes—Biography] I. Title.

E185.96.W38   301.45′19′6073 [B] [920]   74–3154
ISBN 0–8116–4910–5

Contents

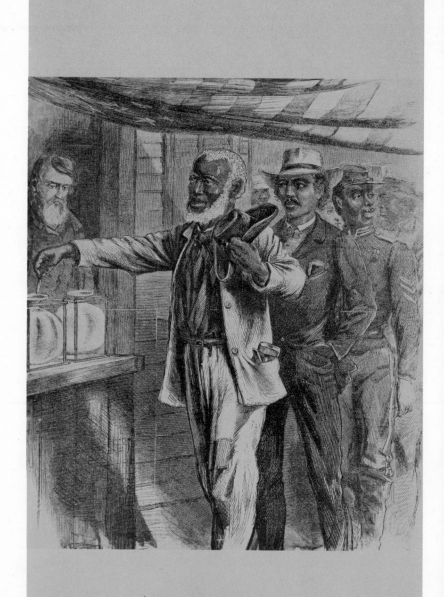

Black Crusaders for Freedom

The fierce battle blacks had fought, first for their freedom from slavery and then for equal rights, seemed to have been won in March 1870 with the passage of the Fifteenth Amendment to the Constitution. Now no man could be denied the right to vote because he was black.

Many Americans had labored mightily for this day. This book is about some of them—black men and women who saw beyond the confines of slavery and were determined to help their people. Sojourner Truth, born a slave in the state of New York, became one of the antislavery movement's most persuasive speakers. Frederick Douglass escaped from slavery to become a great and wise leader of his people. A bold and fiery orator, he bore witness to the cruelties of slavery. Harriet Tubman fled from slavery herself and then courageously returned again and again to the South to lead hundreds of slaves to freedom. Booker T. Washington's passion to learn and then to help other blacks to learn resulted in the founding of the great Tuskegee Institute.

For these Americans—and for the thousands of others who had fought tirelessly to end the terrible institution of slavery—the vote was a giant step forward.

The struggle, of course, was not over. The right to vote would be denied in practice in many parts of the United States. The battle for equal rights would be fought over and over again for a hundred years and more.

But because these first black crusaders had struggled so hard, the battle now would be fought on the basis of a solemn promise given in the Constitution, the nation's most sacred document. In the end, it could not be lost.

SOJOURNER TRUTH
About 1797–1883

She spoke with a passion born of deep
religious belief, this towering woman
with the powerful voice. From town to
town and state to state Sojourner Truth
trudged, speaking out against the cruel
institution of slavery. A runaway slave,
Sojourner knew firsthand the bitterness
of slavery and was determined to bring
the truth to others. With freedom won,
Sojourner Truth now lifted her voice in
the cause of the nation's blacks who
lived, all too often, in poverty and
misery. She demanded for her people
the right to be educated and the right
to earn a living—and she would not be
silenced.

Sojourner Truth
Fearless Crusader

by Helen Stone Peterson

1. God in Heaven

"Why is mama working upstairs so late?" Belle asked her father one cold evening in 1806.

"There must be some trouble," the old man replied uneasily. Sick with chills and fever, he lay on some straw on the rough board floor of the cellar that was their home. Here in the Hudson River valley of New York, a Dutchman named Charles Hardenbergh owned a large farm. The fourteen slaves who belonged to him lived in the damp cellar under his big house.

Belle saw that her father was shivering. "I'll get your medicine, papa," she said in Dutch, the only language she knew. She held her father's head carefully while she gave him the medicine her mother had made from wild roots.

Belle's full name was Isabella, and she was tall for a nine-year-old. Her father was called Bomefree, a Dutch nickname that meant "straight as a tree." By this time, however, the back of the old slave was bent from long years of hard work. He was often sick. He had felt great sorrow too. His first two wives had been sold away from him. His third wife, Mau-Mau Bett, Belle's mother, had had twelve children. However, one by one they were sold away. Now only Belle and her younger brother Peter were left.

Suddenly Belle heard footsteps. She threw a fresh pine log on the fire that supplied both light and heat in the cellar. Mau-Mau Bett entered with Peter, her big hand clutching her son's small one.

"The master is very ill," she burst out. "He's going to die."

Bomefree moaned, "What will become of us?" The other slaves, who had gathered to hear the news, began to moan too.

Mau-Mau Bett sobbed bitterly. "When the master dies, we'll all be sold." She turned to Bomefree. "Our last two children will be taken from us."

Belle was terror stricken. She flung her arms around her mother. "Mama, don't let it happen!" she begged. Belle felt that without her parents she could not go on.

Her father began to mutter. "I knew a master who threw a slave child against a wall and knocked out its brains. An Indian friend of mine said he would have hurled his tomahawk at the murderer's head. He asked me why I didn't kill the master—kill—"

"Stop!" ordered Mau-Mau Bett. "The only way we can go on is by trusting God." She turned to Belle and Peter. "Children, if you are separated from us, talk to God. Listen to the answers he gives you. He will help you."

Belle had often heard her mother speak about God. This evening her words had new importance for the frightened girl. "Mama, tell me where God is," Belle begged.

Mau-Mau Bett led her children outside and pointed to the sky. "God is up there in heaven. Right now he sees all my other children, even though I don't know where they are."

Mau-Mau Bett walked back into the cellar and sat down in a chair. She lifted her son to her lap and drew Belle to her side. Then she began singing African songs her mother had passed down to her. Belle did not understand the words, but she knew some of the songs had happy sounds. Others seemed filled with sorrow. Leaning close against her mother, Belle wept.

Before long, Charles Hardenbergh died. Soon a sale of his possessions was advertised. The notice read: "Slaves, horses, and other cattle will be sold."

On the morning of the sale, a member of the Hardenbergh family made a grand announcement to Belle's parents. He said, "We have decided to set you both free."

The old couple trembled with joy, for they had longed to be free. It saddened them, however, that their children were not freed too. Actually the Hardenberghs had freed them to save money. Now they would not have to look after Bomefree, who was not able to work. Mau-Mau Bett would have to support him.

An American slave market. Belle was separated from her family at a slave sale much like this one.

The sale started off well, and Peter and the other slaves brought good prices. Then it was Belle's turn to stand on the wooden platform and be sold. No one bid for her, though. She had a faraway look in her eyes that made many in the crowd uneasy. "She might not obey," they thought.

The man in charge of the sale shouted, "Get a bargain! Buy this female and I'll throw in a flock of sheep. What will you pay?"

"One hundred dollars," called out John Neely. He was a storekeeper who lived a few miles away. The offer was accepted.

Mr. Neely climbed on his horse and motioned for Belle to walk behind him. Her mother and father came hurrying to say good-bye.

"I'll manage to come see you," Bomefree promised, sobbing.

Tears streamed down Mau-Mau Bett's cheeks. She kissed Belle and whispered, "Talk to God. He will help you."

Mr. Neely rode away. After him trotted the terrified, heartbroken black child.

2. Slave Masters

Mrs. Neely glared at the black girl who followed her husband into the kitchen. "Who's that?" she asked sharply.

"I bought a slave to help you with the housework," her husband answered. The Neelys, who were newcomers in the county, had never before owned a slave.

Mrs. Neely's eyes narrowed. She hated black skin, and this girl's skin was pure black. "What's your name?" she demanded.

Belle stared at her new mistress and did not answer.

"She doesn't speak English, only Dutch," said Mr. Neely. The Neelys did not speak Dutch.

"John Neely, you must have lost your senses," cried his wife.

"Now the war begins," thought Belle, seeing Mrs. Neely's rage.

Dazed and frightened, Belle did not learn English quickly. When Mrs. Neely sent her for the frying pan, she brought back the kettle. When Mr. Neely sent her to the smokehouse for bacon, she brought back a ham.

One Sunday morning everything went wrong. Mr. Neely ordered Belle to the barn. He tied her hands together, and with a thick switch, he whipped the ten-year-old girl until the blood ran down her legs. She sobbed wildly. Mr. Neely whipped her again. When he left the barn, the girl lay in a pool of her own blood.

"I shall get away from here," Belle promised herself, as she struggled to get up.

To her great joy, her father came to see her a few weeks later. Belle managed to leave the house and be alone with him briefly. She showed him the terrible scars from the beating. It had been only one of many. Bomefree could not hold back his bitter tears.

"My poor child, I'll try to find a better master for you," he promised.

Not long afterward Martin Schryver stopped at the house. He was a fisherman who also owned a tavern near the Hudson River. He asked Belle, "Would you like to work for my wife and me?"

"Yes," she replied eagerly. She felt sure her father

had told this man about her. Mr. Schryver bought Belle for $105.

The Schryvers had little money, but they were jolly, easygoing people. While Belle was living with them, she learned to speak English, though she never did learn to read and write. Belle helped unload the fish from Mr. Schryver's boats. She spent sunny hours hoeing in the garden. She grew strong and tall. By the time she was thirteen years old, she stood among other girls like an oak among saplings.

Mr. John Dumont, who had a large estate at New Paltz, saw Belle. He said he wanted to buy her.

"I'm not selling her," Mr. Schryver told him.

"I'll give you three times what you paid for her," offered Mr. Dumont.

"Oh, my goodness," exclaimed Mrs. Schryver. She begged her husband to sell Belle. "We don't own anything else that will bring such a nice profit," she pointed out. The sale was soon arranged.

At the Dumonts' Belle helped with the cooking and did the laundry. She worked in the barn and the fields as well. Mr. Dumont, who owned ten slaves, was very pleased with Belle.

"She does more than six ordinary workers," he told his family.

Mrs. Dumont preferred white house servants, and she had one named Kate. Kate set out to make trouble for the slave girl who had become Mr. Dumont's favorite.

One morning the potatoes that Belle boiled for breakfast looked dirty. "Here's a fine example of Belle's work," snapped Mrs. Dumont.

The potatoes looked dirty a second morning and again on a third morning. Frantic with worry, Belle kicked the cat.

"I'll not have you hurting the cat!" shouted Mr. Dumont. He whipped Belle.

Later that day the Dumonts' daughter Gertrude spoke to Belle. "I hate to have the family so angry at you. I'll try to find out what's happening to the potatoes."

The next morning Gertrude took a book and sat by the kitchen fireplace. Belle put the kettle of peeled potatoes over the fire. Then, as usual, she left to help milk the cows. Before long Gertrude saw Kate slip past her and throw ashes into the kettle.

Gertrude ran to her parents. "I know what's been happening to Belle's clean potatoes." She told the story.

Mrs. Dumont tossed her head and made no comment.

Mr. Dumont exclaimed, "I said Belle is the best worker we ever had. I plan to give her some special privileges."

One day word came that Mau-Mau Bett was dead. Belle was heartsick at the thought that she would never again hear her beloved mother's voice. Mr. Dumont let her ride to the funeral in one of his farm wagons.

Belle found her old father filled with despair. "I thought I'd go before your mother," he cried, clinging to Belle's hand. "What's to become of me?" Bomefree was now badly crippled and nearly blind.

"If I were free, I'd take care of you, papa," sobbed Belle.

For a time some members of the Hardenbergh family tried to look after Bomefree. Then they sent him to live in a lonely cabin in the woods. He was found there one day, frozen to death.

3. Rebellious Slave

When Belle was in her late teens, she fell in love with a handsome young slave named Bob. He worked on a nearby farm. Although Belle was now almost six feet tall, Bob was even taller.

Bob longed to marry Belle, but Mr. Catlin, his master, would not allow it. He said Bob must marry a slave on the home place. One day Bob told Belle that Mr. Catlin had ordered him not to visit her. "But I have to see you. And I shall!" declared Bob.

On a Saturday afternoon a few weeks after this, Belle lay sick on her straw bed. The Dumont slaves all slept together in a one-room shed behind the kitchen. Mr. Dumont stepped into the shed.

"Belle, have you seen Bob?"

"No, master," she said.

"If you do, tell him the Catlins are after him," warned Mr. Dumont.

Suddenly Belle heard a commotion outside. She dragged herself to the window. With horror she saw that Mr. Catlin and his son were beating Bob with heavy canes. His face and head were covered with blood. The Catlins kept pounding him.

"Stop!" called Mr. Dumont. "I'll have no slaves killed here."

The Catlins tied Bob with a rope and led him away.

Belle never saw Bob again. He married one of Mr. Catlin's slaves, and a short time later he died.

Belle felt lost and alone. Then she remembered her mother's words. "The only way we can go on is by trusting God," Mau-Mau Bett had said.

"I must have a secret place where I can talk to God," Belle decided.

She knew of a small island in a narrow stream. On this island she made a clearing, then wove branches into a wall around it. Now she had a room where no person could see her. And no person could hear her voice, for the stream fell over some rocks nearby and made a roaring sound.

In this secret place Belle regularly prayed aloud. Fixing her eyes on the sky, she talked to God.

Here, too, in her deep-toned voice, she sang the African songs her mother had passed down to her. The music filled Belle with warmth and pleasure.

She continued to visit her secret place during the rest of her years with the Dumonts. At Mr. Dumont's command she married Tom, a much older slave on the farm. Mr. Dumont had sold away Tom's two previous wives. Belle had five children—four daughters and a son.

Now when Belle worked in the fields, she took her small children with her. This way she could watch over them. She carried the baby in a basket that she would hang on a bush. Then one of Belle's girls would swing the basket until the baby fell asleep.

While her children were still small, Belle began looking forward joyously to freedom for all her family. In 1817 New York had passed a law that said adult slaves must be set free on July 4, 1827. Children were to stay and serve their masters—girls to the age of 25 and boys to 28. Then they, too, would be free.

Mr. Dumont made Belle a promise. "You have worked so hard that I'll give your freedom to you one year early." He said Tom could also have his freedom then.

In 1826 Belle hurt her hand badly. She continued to work hard, though. Yet on July 4 Mr. Dumont told her, "You can't have your freedom. You didn't do as much work as usual these past months."

"But, master, you promised," protested Belle.

"It's settled," Mr. Dumont said. "You won't be free until next year."

"He lied to me," thought Belle, and she reached a decision. "I shall take my freedom." She was now twenty-nine years old.

Belle talked to her husband. Old Tom's heart thumped with fear as he listened to his strong-minded wife. "I'm staying safely here and so should you," he told her.

Belle went to her secret place and prayed. She made her plans. She stayed to help harvest the crops. Then one morning just before daybreak, Belle picked up her baby Sophia and walked off.

A few miles away she stopped at the home of a Quaker family, Mr. and Mrs. Isaac Van Wagener, whom she knew slightly. Like many Quakers the Van Wageners were against slavery. They received Belle kindly and asked her to stay with them.

Before long Mr. Dumont arrived. "You ran away," he said to Belle.

"No, I took the freedom you promised me," she replied with dignity.

"You must come back," Mr. Dumont ordered.

"No, I shall not," asserted Belle.

Mr. Van Wagener said to Mr. Dumont, "I do not believe in slavery. I will pay what you think is due you, so that Belle and her baby may have their freedom now." Mr. Dumont took $25 and left.

Belle started to thank Mr. Van Wagener. "Master—"

"Don't call me that," said the gentle Quaker. "You have no master but God."

4. "I'll Have My Child"

Belle lived with the Van Wageners and did their housework. She was lonesome for her older children. However, she thanked God she had her baby Sophia with her. For about a year Belle stayed in the Van Wageners' peaceful, quiet home.

Suddenly one autumn day she had horrible news. She learned that her six-year-old son Peter was a slave on a plantation in the South. Mr. Dumont had sold Peter to his neighbors the Gedneys. But then Solomon Gedney had traded Peter to his brother-in-law in Alabama. Now Peter would not be set free at age 28, for Alabama had no such law. This sale across state lines was against the law.

"I must try to get my son back," sobbed Belle.

She left Sophia in the care of the Van Wageners. Then Belle hurried to the Dumonts' farm in New Paltz. She ran a good part of the way. Mr. Dumont was not at home, but Belle poured out her grief to Mrs. Dumont.

Mrs. Dumont's eyes were filled with hate. "A fine fuss to make about a little black boy!"

Belle's eyes flashed. "I'll have my child again!"

"How?" demanded Mrs. Dumont. "You have no money—nothing."

Belle lifted her head proudly. "God will help me," she said. Later Belle told her friends, "I felt as if the power of a nation was within me."

Belle went to a Quaker family in New Paltz. They said she must take her case to the court in Kingston, nine miles away.

At the courthouse in Kingston, Belle talked with an official named Mr. Chip. He drew up a legal paper that ordered Solomon Gedney to appear in court. Mr. Gedney learned about the paper and left at once for Alabama to get Peter.

Belle decided to stay close to the courthouse until Mr. Gedney returned. She earned money by doing housework.

In the spring Mr. Gedney finally came back with Peter. But the next session of court was not till autumn, Mr. Chip told Belle. A panic came over her.

"I must have my son now," protested Belle.

"That's nonsense," snapped Mr. Chip.

As Belle walked away from his office, she wondered what to do. On the street a stranger stopped her. "Did they give your boy to you?" he asked.

Tears sprang to Belle's eyes as she told him of the delay.

The stranger said, "Listen to me. I feel sure that Lawyer Romeyne can get your son for you now." He pointed out the lawyer's house.

Belle knocked on the door, and Mr. Romeyne himself opened it. He stared at the tall, barefoot, black woman. "I must talk with you," Belle cried.

"Come in," said Mr. Romeyne gruffly.

Peter's story tumbled from Belle. "All right, I'll get your son," said the lawyer. "But first I need five dollars to pay a man to go to the Gedneys."

Belle did not have a cent. Once more she walked to New Paltz. Her Quaker friends gave her the money, and she turned it over to Mr. Romeyne. The day after that, Mr. Gedney brought Peter to the courthouse.

When Belle entered the judge's chamber, Peter shouted, "She's not my mother!" Throwing his arms around Mr. Gedney's knees, Peter yelled, "I want to stay with my good master."

The judge saw that there were bad scars on Peter's face. He asked, "What caused that scar on your forehead?"

Peter looked quickly at Mr. Gedney before replying, "A horse kicked me."

Peter was a very frightened boy, the judge realized. He asked more questions and decided that Mr. Gedney had forced the boy to lie. Then he ordered that Peter be given to Belle.

That night when she took off Peter's shirt, Belle saw that his entire back was covered with deep scars. "What's all this?" she asked.

Peter began to sob. "It's where the master down South whipped and kicked me."

Belle gathered her sobbing son into her arms and hugged him tightly.

Belle continued to work in the Kingston area. She found a job for Peter at a place where he could live. She longed to have Peter and Sophia with her. The little girl was still at the Van Wageners'. But the only job Belle could get was as a servant with people who had no room for her children. Mr. Dumont felt a bit sorry about what had happened to Peter. So he took Sophia to live on his farm. There she was looked after by her older sisters, who had to work for Mr. Dumont until they were 25.

Tom had his freedom now, but no one would give

regular work to the old, untrained man. Hunger forced him to enter the poorhouse. There he remained until he died.

It was Belle's great faith in God that brought her through these hard times. She had never been allowed to go to church during her years in slavery. Now she attended the Methodist church in Kingston. Here she met a New York City schoolteacher named Miss Gear, who spent her vacations in Kingston.

"Peter should have an education," Miss Gear told Belle. Though no school in the area took blacks, Miss Gear told Belle that some schools in New York did. "If you will come to the city, I will pay for Peter's education," Miss Gear said. "And I'll find work for you."

"We shall go," Belle decided.

She was sorry to say good-bye to her daughters. Holding back her tears, Belle told the girls, "Someday I hope to have a home where we all can be together."

5. The Kingdom

Belle and Peter moved to New York in 1829. Miss Gear placed the boy in school and found a home for him. She knew a deeply religious family who were pleased to hire Belle to do housework.

This family and their friends often held prayer meetings on street corners. They hoped to turn more people to religion. Belle gladly took part in these services. She was looking for ways to serve God.

During her third year in New York, Belle became housekeeper for Elijah Pierson, a wealthy widower. Mr. Pierson was kind and full of religious zeal.

"God intends to set up his kingdom of love and peace on earth," Mr. Pierson told Belle repeatedly. He spent a great deal of time reading the Bible to her and telling her what it meant. Some of his explanations were strange indeed. He was well known in religious circles for his odd ideas.

New York in 1830. Belle had moved to the big city the year before so that Peter could attend school.

One day there was a knock on the door, and Belle answered it. She saw a man with shoulder-length hair and a beard one foot long. He looked just like the pictures of the prophets that she had seen in the Bible.

"My name is Matthias. I have been sent by God to set up the kingdom of heaven on earth," he said.

"Oh, yes!" gasped Belle. The words rang true to her, for Mr. Pierson had prepared her for them.

The truth was that Matthias had been arrested more than once for disturbing the peace. The authorities had thought he was insane, but he convinced them he was not. Now he convinced Mr. Pierson that he was God's messenger. He won other followers too. Among them were Ben Folger, a well-to-do businessman, and his wife.

Belle, Mr. Pierson, and the rest of the followers moved with Matthias to a country estate. They called it "The Kingdom." It was supposed to be a place where all lived and worked in a spirit of brotherly love. However Belle, the only black person in the group, was kept busy at the hard work. The others had light tasks. Matthias did little except enjoy himself and preach some meaningless sermons. Soon there were jealous quarrels and angry words among his white followers. Love and peace were certainly not present at The Kingdom, Belle realized.

By this time Mr. Pierson was ill in both mind and body. Belle looked after him the best she could. When he died suddenly, The Kingdom broke up. Belle returned to New York.

Relatives of Mr. Pierson said that he had been poisoned. Matthias was arrested and tried for murder but was found not guilty. During the trial the Folgers spread the rumor that Belle had tried to poison them.

"An African witch," a newspaperman wrote of Belle. "She is the most wicked of the wicked."

Belle was stunned. Then, gathering her strength, she made up her mind to fight these untruths.

Her first step was to get proof of her good character. She went back to Kingston. Her past employers in that area wrote letters that highly praised her.

While Belle was trying to think what to do next, a rare thing happened. A white newspaperman by the name of Gilbert Vale came forward to help her. He knew she was being treated unfairly.

"People are prejudiced against her because she is black, poor, and uneducated," he said.

Mr. Vale made a complete investigation. Then he wrote a two-volume book in defense of the former slave.

Meanwhile, with great courage, Belle decided to go to court. She started a suit for slander against the prominent Mr. Folger. He had spread lies, she said, that hurt her reputation. At that time most blacks in the United States were still slaves. It was very unusual for a black person to sue a white one. Yet Belle won the case. The all-white jury awarded her a small sum of money for the damage done to her good name. It was a shining triumph for Belle.

The Matthias affair left her a lot wiser. From then on she never let anyone tell her what the Bible meant. Belle explained, "I talk to God, and God talks to me."

Belle stayed in New York doing housework. As the years went by, she grew more and more troubled about her son Peter. He had quit school. He was often jobless. Now he was getting into trouble.

Peter liked ships. When he consented to go to sea as a sailor, Belle was pleased. She received several letters from him. Then the letters stopped, and Belle never heard from her son again. She feared his ship had been sunk at sea.

Belle was torn with grief over Peter. "He had no childhood, only beatings," she told herself. Her heart was heavy as she thought of all the cruelty and injustice suffered by black people.

Belle's thoughts turned to her daughters. She had visited them as often as she could. But she had not been able to save money to buy a home where they might live with her. Though Belle worked hard, her employers paid her next to nothing.

In New York Belle had seen many people, both black and white, who were even poorer than she was. They often went hungry, and their homes were miserable. How could such poverty be overcome? And how could cruelty and injustice be done away with?

For Belle the true answer lay in God's command: "Do unto others as you would have them do unto you."

Belle thought and prayed. It came to her that God had new work for her to do. She told a friend, "The Lord has given me a new name—Sojourner. I'm to travel up and down the land, to tell people about God's commands."

She packed a few clothes in a pillowcase. Then on a June morning in 1843, Sojourner, now 46 years old, left New York. She started walking toward Long Island to spread God's word.

6. God's Sojourner

Sojourner moved along with brisk steps. Happily she whispered her new name, "Sojourner."

She had no exact plans. But she told herself firmly, "God has work for me to do ahead, bringing his truth to people." In great excitement she spoke aloud. "Truth! My full name will be Sojourner Truth."

That night she stopped at a house and asked to

sleep there. She had no trouble finding places to stay as she continued her journey. Cheerfully she helped with housework or nursing at each stop.

On Long Island and throughout New England at that time, white people were holding religious meetings. Sojourner walked from meeting to meeting, many of which were held outdoors or in tents. Soon she was speaking at them, like a preacher. "To be good in the eyes of God, you must do good to all his children," she would tell the crowds.

By the time Sojourner had reached Springfield, Massachusetts, she was tired. She said to friends, "I'd like to stay awhile in some nice place."

They told her about a cooperative community, or commune, near Northampton, Massachusetts. The members believed in the worth and dignity of every individual. They lived simply. They supported themselves by raising silkworms and weaving silk cloth.

"I'll go to see this place," Sojourner decided.

He heart sank when she saw the ugly brick building where the people lived. It housed the silk factory as well. The group gave Sojourner a warm welcome, however, and she decided to stay. She took on the job of washing the clothes for the community.

She soon learned that most of the adults were abolitionists. They demanded that slavery in the South be abolished, or done away with, at once. Abolitionists were a small minority in the nation, and many Americans hated them. Sojourner met the leaders of the movement when they visited the community. She came to know Frederick Douglass, the escaped slave, who was now lecturing at antislavery meetings.

Sojourner thought, "Does God have work for me to do in freeing the slaves?"

She was still searching for an answer to this question when the community ended. The silk business had not made enough money for the people to live on. Sojourner stayed at Northampton and did housework. One day Olive Gilbert, an abolitionist friend, said:

"People should read of the cruel things you and your family suffered in slavery. Then more of them would be aroused to wipe out this wickedness. Will you talk to me about your life? I will write it down for you in a book."

"Yes, yes," cried Sojourner. She was certain that God had opened the way for her to help free the slaves.

Miss Gilbert wrote the book. It was published in 1850, when Sojourner was 53. "Start traveling to antislavery meetings," Miss Gilbert advised her. "People there will buy your book and read it. Then they will tell others of the evil of slavery."

Sojourner began attending meetings in Massachusetts. She took along copies of her book. People crowded around her to buy them.

One day, at a large outdoor meeting, the chairman called upon Sojourner to speak. As she stood up, it came to her that she would start by singing. She put all her strong feelings into the song she had made up:

> *I am pleading for my people,*
> *A poor downtrodden race,*
> *Who dwell in freedom's boasted land*
> *With no abiding place.*

Sojourner sang several verses, her voice ringing through the treetops. She then began to talk about the suffering of Mau-Mau Bett, Bomefree, and her son Peter. Tears rushed down the faces of many listeners.

The next winter Sojourner traveled through New York State with a group of antislavery speakers. At the meetings Sojourner would sing and tell of the terrible life of the slaves.

"You are committing an awful sin by holding colored people in slavery. You don't know God, and God doesn't know you," Sojourner cried out to white Americans. "When I was a slave, I hated you. But now God has given me love enough so that I love even the white folks. Free my people and save yourselves from being punished by God."

The tour ended in Rochester. Sojourner spent the rest of the winter there with Amy Post, a friend of

Olive Gilbert's. Mrs. Post arranged meetings for Sojourner, who was now becoming well known as a speaker. She was the first black woman to give antislavery lectures in America.

7. Woman's Rights

In the spring Sojourner said good-bye to Mrs. Post. She left to give antislavery lectures in other parts of the country.

Sojourner traveled west. In May she was at Akron, Ohio. A woman's rights convention was being held there.

Sojourner had been told that women were beginning to make an organized fight for justice and equality. At that time a wife's earnings belonged to her husband. And by law their children belonged to him too. Few jobs were open to women, and they could not vote.

"We're trying to change these things," a white friend told Sojourner. "Women must have equal rights with men."

Sojourner agreed that women as well as blacks must win full human rights.

Sojourner walked into the convention at Akron and sat down on a step of the stage. The women in this midwestern city were upset. They feared that their cause would be hurt if it were connected with the antislavery movement, which was still unpopular in their part of the country. They did not want Sojourner to speak.

A number of ministers spoke, arguing against the woman's movement. One shouted angrily, "God did not intend women to have equality with men!" Men in the audience clapped and roared their approval.

Sojourner stood up then and began to speak. "That man over there says that women need to be helped into carriages and lifted over ditches and to have the best place everywhere. Nobody ever helps me into carriages or over mud puddles or gives me any best place."

In a voice that sounded like rolling thunder, she asked, "And aren't I a woman?"

Sojourner bared her right arm to the shoulder and showed her muscles. "I have plowed and planted and gathered into barns, and no man could head me. And aren't I a woman?

"I could work as much and eat as much as a man when I could get it, and bear the lash as well. And aren't I a woman?"

Sojourner said that women were equal to men and should have the same rights. She spoke with humor and power. When she finished, the applause was so loud that the windows rattled. "She . . . turned the whole tide in our favor," wrote the chairman.

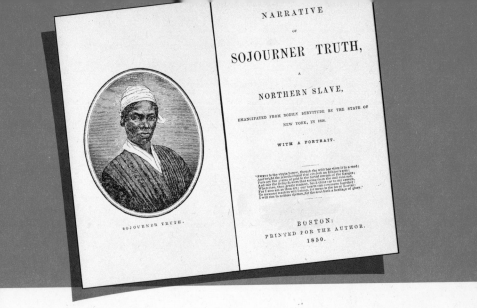

The title page of Miss Olive Gilbert's biography of Sojourner Truth

All the rest of her life, Sojourner was a fighter for woman's rights. She attended many woman's rights meetings and made wonderful speeches.

After the Akron convention, Sojourner stayed in Ohio. She worked for the freedom of the slaves. At first she spoke at meetings planned by antislavery groups. Then for a while she arranged her own meetings. Sojourner borrowed a horse and buggy and drove about alone.

When she came to a crossroads, she would lay down the reins and say, "God, you drive."

The horse would start down one of the roads. Sojourner told a friend, "We always came to some good place where I had a successful meeting."

It was not an easy life, though. White children often called Sojourner names and threw mud at her.

At one meeting a law student leaped to his feet. "Negroes are fit only to be slaves!" he shouted. "If any show intelligence, it's because they have white blood."

Sojourner held her head high. Around her hair, now gray, she wore a white turban in the African style. "I am pure African. You can all see that plain enough," she said with pride. "None of your white blood runs in my veins."

After two years in Ohio, Sojourner traveled back East. That autumn she visited Harriet Beecher Stowe, who lived in Andover, Massachusetts. Mrs. Stowe was the author of *Uncle Tom's Cabin*, a book that had turned many northerners against slavery.

From the first moment, Mrs. Stowe was aware of Sojourner's great inner strength. Her home was full of guests whom she introduced to Sojourner. "No princess could have received a drawing-room with more composed dignity than Sojourner her audience," wrote Mrs. Stowe. "She stood among them, calm and erect, as one of her own native palm trees waving alone in the desert."

Mrs. Stowe later wrote about Sojourner's visit for a magazine, the *Atlantic Monthly*. That article spread Sojourner's fame across the nation and to Europe.

8. Protest against Slavery

Sojourner made her way back to the Middle West, where she lectured against slavery. The sale of her book brought money for her expenses.

Sojourner worked so hard that she began to look old and worn. Whenever she had to rest, she would stay for a short time with friends in Battle Creek, Michigan.

One day she told her friends, "I have enough money to start buying a little house. I believe I shall make my home here."

Perhaps her daughters would like to live in this pleasant place, she thought. She had never forgotten her dream that someday she would have a home where they all could be together. Her daughters were now over 25 and free. They were married, with families of their own. But they were poor, and life was hard for them.

Sojourner bought a small house. To her delight, one by one her daughters, with their husbands and children, came to Battle Creek. They began setting up their own households; however, some members of the family always shared Sojourner's house.

Although she was now a homeowner, Sojourner kept on traveling and lecturing. "Slavery must be destroyed, root and branch," she cried out to her audiences. More and more people in the North were against slavery.

In April 1861 the Civil War started. "Grant freedom to the slaves at once," some abolitionists demanded. When President Lincoln failed to do this, they were angry.

"Have patience," advised Sojourner. "It takes a great while to turn around this great ship of state."

In January 1863 President Lincoln signed the Emancipation Proclamation. It freed the slaves in the rebellious southern states. Sojourner's heart overflowed with joy. She sank to her knees and thanked God.

Just before Thanksgiving that year, Sojourner decided to bring a holiday dinner to the black soldiers training near Detroit.

On Thanksgiving Day Sojourner arrived at the army camp in a carriage. It was loaded with boxes of turkey, ham, mince pie, and nuts. While the feast was being set out for the eager soldiers, Sojourner started singing. She had made up words of her own to the tune of "John Brown's Body":

We are the hardy soldiers
of the First of Michigan,
We're fighting for the Union
and for the rights of man,
And when the battle rages,
you'll find us in the van,
As we go marching on.

9. A Talk with President Lincoln

After the Emancipation Proclamation, Sojourner's thoughts turned to the problems of the newly freed black people. They were coming out of slavery just as she had, with no money and no schooling. They would need help in finding ways to live and support themselves. Did the nation understand this? Sojourner wondered.

The question came back to her over and over. One day in 1864 she made a decision. "I'll go talk with President Lincoln."

Sojourner reached Washington that fall. She went to see Lucy Colman, an abolitionist friend. Mrs. Colman, a white woman, was now running some classes for black children in the city. She thought she could arrange an appointment with the president.

While she waited for the appointment, Sojourner walked around Washington. She was shocked at the awful misery she saw.

The city was crowded with 13,000 homeless blacks. After the proclamation, they had fled from the South and flocked to the capital. They lived in crowded neighborhoods. As many as 12 to 20 persons shared one-room windowless shacks.

Sojourner saw groups of men, their clothes in rags, leaning aimlessly against buildings. These men, who had worked on plantations, could find no jobs in the city.

She saw mothers, with babies clutched in their arms, staring at one another in bewilderment. Some of the women still wore the old dresses of former mistresses.

Skinny little girls and boys searched through the garbage piled high in dooryards for something to eat. The sight filled Sojourner with fear. She knew disease would spread rapidly in this filth.

Sojourner was now 67 years old. But she realized there was new work for her to do. "I must stay in Washington and help these people," she decided.

Mrs. Colman was able to get an appointment with the president. She went with Sojourner to the White House and made the introduction. President Lincoln bowed and shook Sojourner's hand.

"I am pleased to see you," he said with a smile. "I have heard of you many times."

"You are the best president who has ever taken the seat," Sojourner told him.

"I expect you have reference to my having emancipated the slaves in my proclamation," he said earnestly. "But President Washington and some of the other presidents would have done just as I have done, if the time had come."

Sojourner spoke warmly. "I thank God you were the instrument selected by him and the people to do it."

President Lincoln opened a silver box and took out a Bible. On its gold cover was the picture of a slave with his chains falling from him. "This Bible was presented to me by the colored people of Baltimore," said the president.

"It's beautiful," exclaimed Sojourner, looking down at the Bible.

Then she raised her eyes and looked directly at the president. "This government once sanctioned laws that would not permit my people to learn enough to enable them to read this book. And for what?" she protested.

A look of sadness came over the president's face.

He gladly signed Sojourner's "Book of Life." This was a book in which she collected signatures of people important to her.

The president shook Sojourner's hand when he said good-bye. "I will be pleased to have you call again," he said.

Walking away from the White House, Sojourner spoke thoughtfully to Mrs. Colman. "I felt that I was in the presence of a friend. I have faith that President Lincoln will take steps to help my people."

10. The Promise of Justice

Sojourner went to work in Freedmen's Village at Arlington, Virginia. This was across the Potomac River from Washington. Black people, still streaming into the capital area, were now sent to this new village. Life here was a little better than in the poor neighborhoods of Washington. Built on farmland, the village gave families small houses or rooms in barracks.

"We need you as a counselor," the superintendent of Freedmen's Village told Sojourner. Most of the women had a great deal to learn about homemaking. Like their husbands, they had worked on plantation fields from sunrise to dark.

"Be clean! Be clean! Cleanliness is godliness," Sojourner told the women as she walked from one house to another. She taught them how to cook and nurse the sick. And she talked with them about their children.

"Your children must go to school and learn to read," said Sojourner. "Then they can be somebody." The girls and boys eagerly went to classes taught by teachers from the North.

Some of the former slaves who lived in Freedmen's Village

One day Sojourner came upon a group of weeping mothers. She learned that white men from Maryland had taken their children away. They made the children work for them without pay and kept them from school.

"Fight the robbers!" ordered Sojourner. "You're free now. Don't let anyone treat you like slaves. You have rights, and the law will protect you." She helped the mothers make use of the law to get their children back.

One of the men from Maryland went to Sojourner. "Old woman, stay out of our affairs, or we'll put you in jail."

Sojourner glared at him. "If you try anything like that, I shall make the United States rock like a cradle," she snapped. The men left her alone.

As Sojourner carried on her work through the winter, it troubled her to see the large number of men without jobs. She learned, though, that they had bright hopes for the future. They counted on land in the South being given to them. Then they could be self-supporting.

"We blacks worked the land for more than 200 years. Yet we don't own one inch of it, and we don't have a penny," one man told Sojourner. "President Lincoln isn't going to turn us loose like a bunch of stray dogs, with nothing."

"The government has promised 40 acres and a mule to each family. The army officers told us that," said another man. He had fought with the Union army.

Sojourner believed the former slaves should have this land to give them a start. She trusted President Lincoln to help the blacks get what they needed.

That spring, on April 9, 1865, the war ended with victory for the Union. Six days later President Lincoln died from an assassin's bullet.

Stunned by their loss, the people of Freedmen's Village sobbed aloud in the streets. Sorrowfully they all draped their poor homes with black rags. Turning to Sojourner for comfort, they cried, "Mr. Lincoln was our savior."

Sojourner, her eyes filled with tears, nodded in agreement.

Andrew Johnson, who had been vice president, now became president. Sojourner decided she must see him. She asked Mrs. Colman to arrange an appointment. On a Sunday afternoon Mrs. Colman once again went with Sojourner to the White House. She made the introduction.

"Please be seated, Mrs. Truth," said President Johnson.

"Sit down yourself, Mr. President," replied Sojourner politely. "I'm used to standing because I've been lecturing many years."

She spoke about her concern for the future of her people. President Johnson listened courteously. However, he did not say clearly what he planned to do to help black Americans.

11. Freedom Rides

Not long after this, the War Department asked Sojourner to work in Freedmen's Hospital in Washington. It was crowded with black men who had been wounded in the war. There was a serious shortage of nurses.

"I shall be glad to do all I can," Sojourner told the officials. She began her new work at once.

One morning she started for the hospital carrying a heavy sack of fruit. Suddenly she decided to take a streetcar.

When she first arrived in Washington, the horse-drawn streetcars were segregated. Special cars carried signs, saying "Colored Persons May Ride in This Car." Now the signs were gone. A law had been passed to forbid segregation on the streetcars. Blacks were shy, however, about claiming their right to ride in any streetcar they wanted.

Sojourner waved at a streetcar to stop. It went right by. Another streetcar came along, but the conductor paid no attention to Sojourner's signal.

"I want to ride!" she screamed. "I want to ride! I want to ride!"

Drivers stopped their carriages and their wagons to see what the cause of this excitement was. A traffic jam built up, forcing the streetcar to stop. Sojourner jumped in and took a seat.

The conductor glared at her. "Get outside and sit on the platform with the driver."

"I shall not," said Sojourner fearlessly. "I have paid five cents' fare, same as these other people. I intend to keep my seat."

"Do as I tell you or I'll throw you out!" roared the conductor.

"You better not try that, or I'll have the law on you," warned Sojourner. "I know my rights and you can't trample on them." The conductor turned away.

Sojourner was delighted with her victory. Later, walking up the path to the hospital, she promised herself, "I shall keep riding. Before I'm through, the conductors will change their ways."

A few days after that, Sojourner had to cross the city on an errand for the hospital. She waved at a streetcar, but it kept going. She ran after it as fast as she could. When the streetcar stopped to take on some white passengers, Sojourner leaped aboard.

The conductor said angrily, "I have a notion to throw you off."

Sojourner refused to back down. "If you try that, it will cost you more than your car and horses are worth," she cried. The conductor let her stay.

Several weeks later Sojourner battled again with the conductors. She and a white friend, Laura Haviland, had put in a hard day collecting supplies for the wounded black soldiers. Loaded with packages, they started for the hospital. Mrs. Haviland signaled a streetcar, and it stopped. Sojourner climbed quickly into the car.

"Get out of the way and let this lady come in," yelled the conductor.

"I am a lady too," said Sojourner.

He said no more. Soon Sojourner and Mrs. Haviland had to change to another streetcar. As they stepped in, a white passenger objected.

"Get off!" the conductor ordered harshly.

"I shall not," Sojourner answered. The conductor grabbed her shoulder.

"Don't put her out," said Mrs. Haviland.

The conductor asked angrily, "Does she belong to you?"

"No," replied Mrs. Haviland calmly. "She belongs to humanity."

"Then take her and go!" shouted the conductor. He slammed Sojourner against the door, but she refused to leave.

By the time she reached the hospital, she was in great pain. Physicians found that her shoulder had been badly hurt. Sojourner went to the police, and the conductor was arrested. He lost his job.

After that, conductors in Washington changed their ways. They stopped the streetcars to take on black people who wanted to ride.

12. Last Protest

Conditions at Freedmen's Hospital improved. So Sojourner decided to find out what she could do to help black refugees in the shacks in Washington. By now the government had opened soup houses in some of the poorest neighborhoods. Here parents stood in line to get food for their hungry families.

One winter day Sojourner went to a soup house. She saw a woman burst into tears. She had been handed one slice of bread and a quart of soup made from dried turnips and potatoes. "That's all the food I have for seven people," the woman wept. "My children are starving to death."

Sojourner visited this woman and her neighbors in their shacks. The shacks were freezing cold. Each family was allowed only two sticks of wood a day. Sojourner learned that in just one alley, four children had recently died.

Men sat around idle. "I'm so tired of doing nothing. It makes me feel no account," one man told Sojourner. The government had not given the 40 acres and a mule that the freed slaves had counted on. There had been no distribution of land. The blacks felt cheated and discouraged.

"These people are being destroyed in body and spirit," thought Sojourner. "They must be helped to escape to a new way of life."

She prayed, "Show me the way, God."

An answer came to Sojourner. She thought of the land in the West owned by the federal government. Much of the land was still unsettled. She wanted the government to give it to the newly freed slaves and let them form communities there. The government should build houses, schools, and hospitals. It should give the men tools for farming, Sojourner decided. With this start, the black people could become self-supporting. They could learn how to manage their own affairs.

Sojourner had a friend write a paper that asked Congress to do these things. Then in February 1870 she traveled to Providence, Rhode Island. There, before a large group of white people, Sojourner told about the terrible conditions in Washington. She asked people to sign the paper she planned to send to Congress.

"Slavery kept my people poor. Give them land and a fair chance to work and get an education," pleaded Sojourner. "Do it and God will bless our country."

When Sojourner finished speaking, men and women pushed forward to sign the paper. After a few more meetings, Sojourner hurried back to Washington.

She delivered the petition to the United States Senate. Fifteen senators left their seats and came to the reception room to shake her hand. Later, one explained the Senate's view of what she asked. "It's an expensive program."

"This nation owes money to the empty-handed colored people for all their unpaid labor," protested Sojourner.

"Congress will do what the majority of Americans demand," said the senator.

"Then I shall go stir up a majority," said the spirited lady of seventy-three years.

Carrying many copies of the petition, Sojourner left Washington. She began lecture tours throughout the North and the Middle West. Her grandson Sammy Banks, a young man of 20, went with her. To help pay their way, she sold photographs of herself.

At her meetings Sojourner asked people to back her program to help the suffering blacks. After hearing her moving talk, most listeners willingly put their names on the paper. Friends along the way took

Sojourner sold this picture of herself to pay the cost of her lecture tours. The poster below announces one of her meetings.

FREE LECTURE!

SOJOURNER TRUTH,

Who has been a slave in the State of New York, and who has been a Lecturer for the last twenty-three years, whose characteristics have been so vividly portrayed by Mrs. Harriet Beecher Stowe, as the African Sybil, will deliver a lecture upon the present issues of the day,

At   **On**

And will give her experience as a Slave mother and religious woman. She comes highly recommended as a public speaker, having the approval of many thousands who have heard her earnest appeals, among whom are Wendell Phillips, Wm. Lloyd Garrison, and other distinguished men of the nation.

☞ At the close of her discourse she will offer for sale her photograph and a few of her choice songs.

charge of sending copies to Congress. Sojourner dreamed of getting so many signatures that Congress would have to act.

After a while her audiences became smaller, however. Sojourner had to face the fact that most Americans wanted to forget the problems of the blacks.

"You don't care about colored people, but God does. They are going to be a people among you!" Sojourner cried out to white Americans.

Her lonely, heroic fight to force Congress to help her people ended after four years. Sammy fell ill, and they returned to Battle Creek where this beloved grandson died. Sojourner herself became very ill, but her daughters nursed her back to health.

In her last years Sojourner went on speaking for the rights of women and black Americans. In one year alone she lectured in 36 towns in Michigan. "Stretch out your hand in brotherhood to the colored people," she begged her white listeners. "We are all the children of one Father in heaven."

In 1883, when Sojourner was 86 years old, she was stricken with a fatal illness. Her daughters took care of her in her home at Battle Creek. "I have done the best I could," Sojourner murmured toward the end. Though she was in great pain, a light filled her face.

Sojourner whispered, "I have told the whole truth."

FREDERICK DOUGLASS
1817–1895

It was clear to see that Frederick
Douglass was not an ordinary man the
very first time he stepped in front of an
audience. The escaped slave bore
himself with such dignity and spoke so
eloquently of his suffering as another
man's property that he moved his
listeners to tears. Frederick Douglass
had found the cause to which he would
devote his life—the freeing of his
people. Danger was never far as he
traveled about the country tirelessly,
pleading with white audiences to put
an end to slavery. The great orator
lived to see his dream of freedom
come true and to lead black Americans
in another struggle—the fight for equal
rights.

Frederick Douglass
Freedom Fighter

by Lillie Patterson

1. Grandma Betsey's Fred

Fred woke suddenly from a sound sleep. Someone leaned over his pallet in the darkness.

"Sh," the woman whispered softly. "It's your mamma."

Fred hugged her. "Can you stay with us this time, Mamma Harriet?"

"No, son. But I had to see you, if just for a little while." She smoothed Fred's curly black hair and kissed him. Her cheeks were wet with tears. "Don't forget me, honey. And don't ever forget your name: Frederick Augustus Washington Bailey. It's a grand name. It was all I could give you."

Fred had seen his mother only a few times in his seven years. Harriet Bailey was a slave and worked on a plantation twelve miles away. To see Fred, she had to walk twelve miles after working in the fields all day. She had to walk the long way back to be in the fields by sunup.

Fred lived with his grandmother, Betsey Bailey. She did not work in the fields, but cared for the small children of slave mothers. Her cabin sat at the edge of a plantation on the Eastern Shore of Maryland.

The morning after his mother's visit, Fred helped Grandma Betsey in her vegetable garden.

"Grandma?"

"Yes, Fred."

"Why can't Mamma Harriet stay with us?"

"She has to do what Old Master tells her to do."

"Who is this Old Master you're always talking about?"

Grandma Betsey sighed. "I'll tell you about him one day."

"Tell me now, grandma."

So Grandma Betsey sat under a tree and talked to Fred about slavery.

"The Old Master is Captain Aaron Anthony. He owns the mothers of the children here. He owns the children too."

Fred hugged his grandmother. "Well, he doesn't own me. I belong to you."

Grandma Betsey took Fred's face in her hands. "He owns me, you, this cabin, everything here. I hate to see you growing. Soon as you are able to work, he'll take you away from me."

"Don't let him take me, grandma."

"Don't you worry, honey." Grandma Betsey looked into the bright spring sky. "Better days are coming for us."

That spring of 1824 passed into summer. Fred

fished with Grandma Betsey as the two talked and sang together. He watched the boats with white sails and dreamed of sailing with them.

One morning Grandma Betsey took Fred's hand. "We're going for a walk."

They walked for miles. It was late afternoon when they came to a large plantation. They walked up a long drive, passed a big house, and came to some small cabins. Children played about them.

"Go and play with the children," Grandma Betsey told Fred. Her face was sad. She hugged him hard and walked away without looking back.

Fred stayed with the children for a time. Then a little girl ran to him. "Grandma Betsey's gone. She left you."

"Grandma Betsey!" Fred screamed. He threw himself to the ground and sobbed. He knew now why he was here. His happy days with Grandma Betsey were over. It was time to go to work as a slave.

2. Great House Farm

Fred spent the next three weeks crying for Grandma Betsey and learning about the Lloyd plantation. Edward Lloyd was one of the richest men in Maryland. He owned over 1,000 slaves and many plantations. The Lloyd family lived in the big mansion on this farm. Slaves called it "Great House Farm."

The plantation was like a country village. Fred's owner, Captain Anthony, was manager of the Lloyd plantations. He, too, lived at Great House Farm.

Captain Anthony put Fred in one of the cabins under the care of an old cook. Fred swept the walks and yards. He chased chickens and ducks out of the gardens. He drove the cows from the pastures at sunset.

Great House Farm was beautiful. Fred loved its beauty, though he missed Grandma Betsey. But then something happened to make him hate the farm.

It was early morning. Fred awoke to the sound of screaming. He peeped through a big crack in the cabin. "It's the slave traders," someone cried. Fred crept outside to see better.

A mother hugged her little girl. "No!" she screamed. "You can't take her."

Then Captain Anthony pulled the child away.

The mother ran to the traders. "Oh, please! Buy me too. She's all I've got."

The buyers went on counting money. They paid several hundred dollars for each slave bought. Then they marched the slaves out of the yard.

"They're going to the Deep South," the mother cried. "I'll never see my little girl again."

During the next months, Fred learned other horrors of slavery. He saw slaves whipped.

When Fred was eight, his mother died. No one told him she was sick. No one took him to see her.

"I hate slavery," Fred whispered every day.

He thought of the life in the Great House. The Lloyds ate the best foods. They dressed in silks and rode in fine carriages. They had dozens of servants.

Then he thought of life in the slave cabins. Slaves were packed together in these huts. They worked from sunup to sunset, in all kinds of weather. Their main food was cornmeal and fat meat or fish. The children all ate from a wooden tray, using oyster shells for spoons. Fred was always hungry.

A typical slave cabin of pre-Civil War times. Fred lived, as a boy, in quarters similar to these.

Children under ten wore only a shirt that hung down to their knees. They never got shoes, stockings, pants, coats, or blankets for cold weather. Fred had to sleep in a closet near the fireplace. In winter he stuck his feet in the warm ashes to keep them from freezing.

"Why am I a slave?" Fred asked himself. "Why are some people slaves and others masters?"

One day Miss Lucretia came to visit her father, Captain Anthony. She was married, but everyone still called her Miss Lucretia.

She needed someone to run errands. Fred came. "What lively eyes you have!" she told him. "And such nice manners."

Fred helped her each day. Miss Lucretia liked to hear him sing. The two played a game. Whenever Fred was hungry, he stood under her window and sang. She would laugh and hand him bread and butter.

One day Miss Lucretia sent for Fred. "I have wonderful news," she said. "You're going to the city of Baltimore. My husband's brother needs someone to care for his little boy. Go and wash. I have a pair of pants for you."

"Oh, thank you!"

Fred gave a great whoop of joy and ran quickly down to the river. He sang as he rubbed all the dirt away. "I must be clean, must be clean for Baltimore."

Fred left that Saturday. As the boat sailed away, he looked back at Great House Farm. Then he turned his face toward Baltimore.

Great adventures lay ahead. Fred could feel it.

3. Baltimore and Books

Fred found Baltimore more exciting than he had dreamed. Fancy carriages rolled along the busy streets. Big ships came and left for places around the world. Tall red-brick buildings with white stone steps stood in rows.

His happy days with the Auld family began. He looked after young Tommy and ran errands. Mrs. Auld treated him almost as a member of the family.

One morning she said, "It's time to study your ABCs, Tommy. You may listen, Fred."

Each morning Fred listened and watched while Tommy learned. Soon he knew the ABCs as well as Tommy. Mrs. Auld began teaching them together. Soon they learned to spell words.

Mr. Auld came home one day during the lesson. "What is going on?" he asked angrily.

Mrs. Auld laughed. "I'm so proud of Freddy. He can read as well as Tommy."

"Stop this at once!" Mr. Auld shouted. "Never teach a slave to read. Once he can read, he will want to be free."

Mrs. Auld stopped the teaching. But Fred did not stop learning. "I'll teach myself," he decided. He made friends with the white boys who lived nearby. He asked them questions about school. He found an old speller and studied in secret. The boys became Fred's teachers. The street became his schoolhouse.

By the time Fred was twelve, he could read very well. He watched for scraps of newspapers or magazines and hid them in his pocket.

Fred earned pennies helping friends shine shoes. When he had saved 50¢ he bought a book he had seen the others reading. *The Columbian Orator* was a book of speeches about liberty. Fred practiced the speeches aloud. He liked the grand thoughts about freedom.

Fred listened carefully when anyone talked about slavery. One day he heard Mr. Auld and friends talking angrily. "Those abolitionists are helping the slaves run away!"

Fred was excited. Who were the abolitionists? Did they really help slaves? He finally found his answer in an old newspaper. The abolitionists were people working to abolish, or end, slavery in the South. The northern states had already abolished slavery.

This news gave Fred hope. There were white men who hated slavery too. He kept on reading and writing in secret. And he began thinking about escaping to freedom.

4. "Let Me Be Free"

"Step lively, Fred. Work faster."

Fred heard this from dawn to dusk. He was now sixteen and had a new owner. Captain Anthony was dead. So was Miss Lucretia. Fred belonged to Thomas Auld, Miss Lucretia's husband. He lived in St. Michaels, an oyster-fishing village down in Talbot County, Maryland.

Thomas Auld was mean to his slaves and never gave them enough to eat. He did not like Fred because Fred was not afraid to speak his mind.

"City life has spoiled you," Thomas Auld told Fred. "I'll have to send you to a slave breaker."

Masters often sent troublesome slaves to slave breakers. These men worked and whipped the slaves until they became easier to manage. So Fred went to the farm of Edward Covey.

Fred had never been a field slave. He did not know how to handle farm tools and animals. The first week Covey said, "Go get a load of wood. Take the cart and two oxen. Hurry!"

Fred finally got the load of wood. But the oxen ran away with the cart. Fred did not know how to stop them. Crash! They ran into the gate, breaking cart and gate.

Covey dashed over to a tree and cut three long switches. "Take your clothes off," he ordered Fred.

Fred stood stubbornly, not moving.

Covey ripped Fred's clothes off. The switches made long red marks across Fred's skin. He clenched his teeth together and would not cry out or beg Covey to stop.

Over the next six months, Covey whipped Fred at least once every week.

Fred worked until he nearly dropped, in rain, snow, hail, and heat. He grew silent. He never smiled.

Covey laughed. "At last I've broken him."

Early one morning Fred went to the barn to feed the horses. Covey sneaked up behind him with a long rope. Suddenly Fred's eyes flashed. Then he doubled his fist. He was seventeen now, tall and powerful.

"Are you going to resist me?" Covey asked, hardly believing what he saw.

"Yes, sir. I don't want to fight you, Mr. Covey. But I won't let you whip me this time."

Covey leaped at Fred like a tiger. But Fred was

like a lion. He held Covey in his strong hands. The two began to give blow for blow. They rolled out of the barn door onto the ground. Covey finally gave up.

"I am a man," Fred told himself. "No master will ever whip me again."

Covey was ashamed to let people know that a young slave had beaten him. He did not report Fred to anyone. He was glad when Auld hired Fred out to another farmer.

On this farm Fred made close friends with other slaves. He taught them in secret to read. He talked to them about freedom.

Fred and five slaves decided to run away. "We'll borrow a canoe and paddle up Chesapeake Bay," Fred planned. "Then we'll go northward on foot. The night before Easter will be a good time."

"How will we know where we're going?" one slave asked.

"We'll follow the North Star. It will guide us to the free states."

On Saturday morning men with guns rode up to the farm. They had found out about the runaway plan. The slaves were put in jail.

"What will happen now?" Fred wondered.

The Aulds of Baltimore saved him. Hugh Auld begged his brother to send Fred back to him.

5. Escape

Fred went to work in a Baltimore shipyard. He learned quickly and soon became a skillful worker.

Every week Fred got paid. He could not spend the money, though. A slave's earnings belonged to his owner.

It was at the shipyard that Fred met Stanley, the sailor. Stanley was a free black man. All blacks in the South were not slaves. Some were born free. Some were freed by their masters. Some worked long years to buy their freedom.

"Every Sunday night the free Negroes get together," Stanley told Fred. "We teach each other what we know. I'll take you to one of our meetings."

Fred went. Everyone liked him. He studied with the group each week. And he began walking home with one of the girls after the meetings. She was Anna Murray. Her calm face and long black hair made Fred think of an Indian princess.

One night Fred whispered, "I'll be free soon, Anna."

"How, Fred?"

"I have a plan. If you miss me, don't worry."

"Be careful, Fred. They'll kill you if you're caught."

Fred planned carefully, step by step. First, he needed money. He got Auld to let him "hire out" his time. Owners sometimes let slaves pay them a sum each week, and keep for themselves any money left over. Fred worked early and late, Sundays and holidays.

One night Anna surprised him. She put some money in his hand. "Take it, Fred. I've been saving too. You find freedom. Then send for me."

Next, Fred needed "free papers." Free blacks had to carry papers to prove that they were not slaves. Stanley had the answer. He offered Fred his "seaman's protection." "This paper protects Negro seamen anywhere," Stanley told Fred. "I'll lend you my sailor's suit and hat too. You can mail them back to me."

One Monday morning in 1838, Fred left home early. He did not go to work, though. He went to Stanley's room. When he came out, he was a handsome sailor, ready for travel.

Fred knew that blacks were checked carefully at train stations. He timed his arrival for the last minute. The engine chugged. Fred dashed up and jumped on the train as it began to move.

"So far, so good," Fred told himself.

He knew the dangers ahead, though. Suppose someone on the train knew him? Suppose the conductor saw that the description on Stanley's paper did not match him?

Luckily the train was crowded. The conductor had to work fast. "Where is your ticket?" he asked Fred.

"I was too late to get one, sir. I'll pay for it now."

"I suppose you have your free papers with you?"

Fred spoke boldly. "Well, sir, I have a paper with an American eagle on it. That will carry me anywhere."

The conductor looked quickly at the paper and gave it back.

Fred was still not safe. Every time the train stopped for more passengers, he held his breath. At one station he looked up and his heart jumped. A German blacksmith who knew Fred well came aboard. The two looked into each other's eyes for a long moment. Then the blacksmith went on to the next car.

"He knows I'm running away," Fred thought. "And he's letting me go."

The train soon reached Wilmington, Delaware. This was a danger spot for Fred. Passengers had to leave the train and take a steamboat for Philadelphia. Wilmington was on the border between slave states and free states. The slave catchers were all about. These spies searched for runaway slaves. Masters paid them for each slave they caught.

But Fred's luck held. He reached Philadelphia and took another train. The next morning he was in New York.

He had escaped. Fred later wrote, "A new world had opened upon me."

But where could he go? Fred walked the streets until night. Then he crept behind some barrels on the waterfront. He slept soundly, the sweet sleep of freedom.

6. New Name—New Life

Once again a friendly sailor helped Fred. The sailor took him to the home of David Ruggles, a black man.

Ruggles listened to Fred's story. "You'll have to hide," he said. "There are some slave catchers even in the North. I'll hide you here while we send for Anna."

"But we are strangers," Fred said. "Why are you helping us?"

Ruggles smiled. "I am free and well educated. So I work to help others get their freedom. Do you know about the Underground Railroad?"

"Very little, sir."

Ruggles explained. "More and more slaves began escaping to free states. Their masters were puzzled. How could they suddenly disappear? Who helped them? One statesman said, 'They go as if swallowed up by an underground road.' So the secret system of helping slaves travel to freedom became known as the Underground Railroad."

"And you help these runaways, Mr. Ruggles?"

"Yes. We are called 'conductors.' Our homes are

the 'stations.' We hide the slaves in our cellars, attics, and barns. We guide them from station to station until they reach freedom. Some settle in northern cities, where the abolitionists help to keep them safe from slave catchers. Others go to Canada. Slave catchers cannot kidnap them there. Canada does not allow slavery."

Anna came, and she and Fred were married. Ruggles told them his plans. "I'll send you to a friend in New Bedford, Massachusetts. That's a busy seaport, and Fred can find work."

Abolitionists helped Fred and his wife slip off to New Bedford by ship.

In New Bedford the couple went to the home of Nathan Johnson, a free black man. "We'll help you get settled," Johnson said. "But first you must have a new name. Then your owner cannot trace you." Johnson looked at Fred's tall, proud figure and smiled. "I know. I'm reading a book called *The Lady of the Lake*. There's a brave man in it named Douglass."

"Douglass." Fred whispered the name. "Frederick Douglass." He said it louder. "That's a grand name for a new life."

Fred and Anna rented a small house. Then Fred went to the shipyard. "I am a first-class shipworker," he told the owner. "I see you need help."

"I'm sorry," the owner answered him. "The workers won't let us hire blacks."

Fred was stunned. "I'll show them," he told Anna. "I'm young, I'm strong, and I'm my own master. Nothing can stop me now."

Fred dug cellars, swept chimneys, and loaded ships. No job was too hard. Later, he got work in a factory.

In New Bedford, Fred read his first copy of the *Liberator*. This newspaper was trying to help end slavery.

The editor of the *Liberator* was William Lloyd Garrison. One day Garrison came to New Bedford to speak. He preached that all men were brothers. Garrison became Douglass's hero.

Abolitionists like Garrison belonged to groups that fought slavery. One group planned a big meeting in Nantucket, Massachusetts, in 1841.

"How I would like to go!" Douglass told Anna.

"Take a holiday," Anna begged. "You've never had one in your life."

Douglass went to Nantucket. He did not dream that the meeting would change his life.

7. The Young Orator

Hundreds of people came to the meeting. Douglass sat near the back of the hall. One of the abolitionists came over. "We want you to say a few words, Mr. Douglass."

"Me? Oh, no!"

"Please. Tell us about slavery."

Douglass trembled as he moved to the platform. He had never spoken to a group of white people before.

The faces were friendly. "What a handsome man!" some people whispered. Douglass was over six feet tall and straight as an arrow. Black curly hair swept back from his broad forehead.

Garrison touched his arm gently. "Tell us your story, Frederick."

The words came easily once Douglass got started. He told how slaves prayed and sang about freedom.

The audience hung on every word. "Go on! Go on!" they cried. Many wept.

When Douglass finished, Garrison stood up. "Have we been listening to a thing, a piece of property, or to a man?"

"A man! A man!" everyone stood up and shouted.

"Come and travel with us," the abolitionists begged Douglass after the meeting. "Make speeches. Tell people how slavery really is."

Douglass and Anna were overjoyed. "Go with them," she said. "I have our babies for company." They now had a girl and a boy, Rosetta and Lewis.

Douglass read books and practiced hard to become a good speaker. He knew his new job would take skill and courage. Even in the North, many people felt that the abolitionists were stirring up trouble. Abolitionists were beaten, jailed, and even killed.

One night Douglass was in a western town. The townspeople would not let him speak in a public building. That did not stop him. He spoke from a platform at the edge of the woods. A crowd came. What a wonderful actor and storyteller he was! He made people laugh one minute and cry the next. His deep-set eyes flashed like fire, and his voice thundered like a trumpet.

Suddenly 30 men dashed up, waving clubs. An egg hit Douglass's face. A brick crashed against his arm.

Frederick Douglass used his newly found talent as an orator to tell the world of the horrors of slavery in America.

"Kill him!" someone shouted. The angry mob beat Douglass and broke his hand. They left him lying on the ground.

Kind friends nursed Douglass until he was well. He was beaten time and time again. But nothing stopped him from speaking out against slavery.

Douglass became such a good speaker that some people began to say, "He was never a slave. He is only pretending."

To stop such talk, Douglass wrote the story of his life: *Narrative of the Life of Frederick Douglass, an American Slave.* In it he named his former owner. That caused trouble for him. The Aulds demanded that their slave be returned.

"Leave the country at once," friends begged. Douglass escaped to England a few hours before slave catchers came for him.

In England, Ireland, and Scotland big crowds came to hear him whenever he spoke. "Stay with us," the English begged. "Send for your family."

Douglass thanked them. "America is my home. I must go back and help to end slavery."

English friends collected $700 to pay Hugh Auld for Douglass's freedom. They collected $2,100 to help Douglass with his work.

After 21 months, Douglass returned home, a free man.

8. *The North Star*

The small room on Buffalo Street buzzed with excitement. Douglass sat at a desk in one corner. A printing press and cases of type filled most of the room.

Douglass's three oldest children worked with him. Rosetta, now eleven, checked a list of names. Lewis and Frederick, Jr., helped two printers set type.

"Do we have any new customers?" Douglass asked Rosetta.

Rosetta's big eyes were bright with happiness. "Five, father. People are really buying our newspaper."

Later, Anna came in with the two youngest children. "We brought you some lunch," little Charles said.

Baby Annie ran over to her father and kissed him. She was only two, and the pet of the family. Douglass loved her dearly.

Lewis brought over a newspaper. "Look! Here's our first copy for this week."

Douglass took the paper. He read the name printed in big type at the top: *The North Star.*

Douglass's big dream had come true. He had used the money his English friends collected to start a newspaper. He had moved his family to Rochester, New York. "I'll fight slavery with my pen, as well as with my voice," Douglass said. "This paper will help to lead the Negro out of slavery."

He thought of the runaway slaves who knew nothing about the geography of the country. The North Star led them toward free states. Often they sang:

I kept my eye on the bright North Star,
And thought of liberty.

So Douglass named his newspaper the *North Star*. It came out once a week. All the family helped with the paper.

The *North Star* gave blacks hope. It told of slaves escaping to freedom, and of friends working to end slavery. It printed stories and poems by black writers.

Douglass used the *North Star* to help all people who were fighting for equal rights. In those days, women did not get the same schooling as men. They could not hold government offices, and they could not vote.

A group of women began to speak for more equality. Most men laughed at them. They called men who helped the women "Aunt Nancy Men." But Douglass was not afraid to help.

In 1848, Douglass went to one of their meetings. Their leader said, "We want the right to vote." Her name was Elizabeth Cody Stanton.

"That's going too far," other women told her.

Mrs. Stanton whispered to Douglass, "Help me. They will listen to you."

Douglass made a speech. His voice flowed over the room like the music of an organ. "Slavery for women is as bad as slavery for Negroes."

Douglass spoke and wrote for many years. Once he made a speech before the New York legislature. One of the legislators whispered to his friend, "I would give twenty thousand dollars, if I could deliver that address in that manner."

9. Railroad Running in Rochester

Songs filled the summer evening. A crowd of children sat in the front room of Douglass's big house on Alexander Street. Rosetta played the piano. Douglass played the violin. Everyone joined in the singing. Then Douglass taught two boys to whistle through their fingers.

Douglass loved children. He loved music, and had taught himself to play the violin. He said, "No man can be an enemy of mine who loves the violin."

Later that night, Douglass heard a rapping at the window, *rat-tat-tat*.

"Who's there?" he asked.

"A friend with friends."

This was the secret greeting of the Underground Railroad conductors. They sent messages in code and sign language.

This handbill notified the members of the Underground Railroad of the safe arrival of twenty-nine runaway slaves in Canada.

A boy stood outside. "Good evening, Mr. Douglass. My father sent a barrel of apples."

"Where are the apples?"

"In our farm wagon."

The "apples" were really runaway slaves. Two teenage boys came in, their hats pulled down around their ears. "We've been walking and hiding for a week," one said.

Douglass took them to a secret room. His whole family was now awake. When the runaways took off their hats, everyone was surprised. The runaways were girls.

"We knew that the slave catchers would hunt for two girls," they explained. "So we cut our hair and dressed as boys."

"Come, Rosetta," Anna said. "They need food and a good rest."

The Douglass home was an important Underground Railroad station. Rochester was on Lake Ontario just across from Canada. Douglass's family helped in running the Railroad, just as they helped in running the paper.

The work had to be done in secret. The government had passed a strict slave law. Anyone caught helping runaway slaves could be fined or put in prison.

The next day, the two oldest Douglass boys collected money and clothes to help the runaways. That night, they took them on to the next station.

Their father was worried about the millions of slaves still in the South. He made friends with a man named John Brown who worried about them too.

Brown often visited the Douglass family. Gentle Annie called him her second father. She followed him around and sat on his knee to listen to stories.

Brown believed that slaves could hide in the mountains of Virginia. But first they must be freed. "God has sent me to free the slaves," Brown decided.

One night in 1859 Brown sent for Douglass. "It's

time for action," Brown began. He unrolled a map. "This is the spot. I can get guns there. I'll need guns to arm the slaves."

"No!" Douglass cried. "That's Harpers Ferry, the government arsenal. You'll be killed." Douglass talked a day and a night. Nothing could make Brown change his mind.

"Come with me, Douglass," Brown pleaded. "I will defend you with my life."

"No, friend. I must fight slavery in my own way."

Brown understood. The two friends parted sadly.

Brown and his followers, among them his own sons, did capture the arsenal. But all of them were killed or taken prisoner. Brown was hanged for plotting against the government.

Letters showed that Douglass knew some of Brown's plans. Again Douglass escaped to England to save his life. But sad news brought him home again. His darling Annie was heartbroken over Brown's death. She worried about what might happen to her father. She lost the power to speak. Soon she died.

"The light and life of my house is gone," Douglass cried. The deaths of Brown and Annie made him hate slavery more than ever.

Brown became a hero to many. The time for action *had* come. Abraham Lincoln was president. The Civil War between the North and the South began.

10. A Day for Poetry and Song

January 1, 1863, was a cold, snowy day in Boston, Massachusetts. Douglass waited there for news from the White House. Would President Lincoln sign the Emancipation Proclamation? This act would free the slaves in the South.

Northern cities were planning grand celebrations. Boston planned the biggest one. Douglass met with a crowd in a large hall. Messengers stayed at the telegraph office to bring the news. All day the crowd waited. No news came.

Darkness fell. Hours passed—eight, nine, ten o'clock. The people began to say, "Lincoln has changed his mind." Douglass tried to cheer them.

Suddenly a messenger ran inside. "It's coming. It's on the wires."

The people sprang to their feet. A second messenger waved a telegram. Lincoln had signed the proclamation. The crowd went wild. Cheers and tears mixed with shouts and sobs.

"Free! Free at last!"

Douglass cried and shouted with them. His rich voice finally turned the shouting into singing: "The year of jubilee is come!"

No one wanted to sleep that night. The celebration went on till dawn. In fact, it went on for the whole year. Douglass spoke at hundreds of joyful jubilee meetings. "We must help the Union win the war," he said.

"Let Negroes fight," Douglass begged the government. The army finally agreed. Douglass traveled from city to city to get black troops.

"I'll sign up," his son Charles said. "I want to be first."

"I'll be second," Lewis said. Later, Fred, Jr., joined too.

In May 1863, 1,000 Negro troops marched down the streets of Boston. It was a proud day for Douglass.

This company of black soldiers was photographed in front of their barracks at Fort Lincoln.

But Douglass became angry when he found out that black soldiers got less pay than white soldiers. They got little care as prisoners, and no promotions to better jobs.

"I must see President Lincoln at once," Douglass said. He went to the White House.

Lincoln smiled and held out his hand. It was the beginning of a true friendship. Lincoln often asked Douglass for advice. "My friend Douglass," Lincoln called him.

The war ended. But soon afterward, President Lincoln was killed. Later, Douglass received one of Lincoln's walking sticks, with a note from Mrs. Lincoln. "My husband often spoke of sending you a gift of friendship." Douglass treasured the gift more than any other he received from famous people.

Friends asked Douglass, "Will you stop and rest now? The Negro is free. You have been fighting for 25 years."

"The fight is only beginning," he told them. "Negroes must have full citizenship and the right to vote. Each Negro must be able to earn a living. Schools, churches, colleges must be opened to all."

Some said, "But Negroes are not ready for this equality."

"*We* are ready," Douglass thundered. "It is you who are not."

11. The Sage of Anacostia

March 4, 1881, was an exciting day in Washington, D.C. James A. Garfield was the new president of the United States. Thousands of people lined the streets to see him.

Garfield stood in front of the Capitol building and took the oath of office. He gave a speech. A tall man stood beside him. The man's hair and beard were snow-white, but his figure was straight and proud.

"That's Marshal Douglass," the people whispered.

Frederick Douglass had been given the job of marshal for the District of Columbia. One of his duties was to escort the new president when he took office.

Douglass and Anna had moved to Washington, D.C. Their children were married and had children of their own. Douglass bought a 20-room house in Anacostia, overlooking the Potomac River and the dome of the Capitol. He called his home "Cedar Hill" because of the many cedar trees. It is now part of the park system in Washington.

Douglass was still busy. He wrote and spoke for the Irish and Chinese of America who were treated unfairly. He worked to help poor people. He even helped to get better treatment for animals. "I have worked hardest to get equal rights for Negroes," he said. "But this does not keep me from working to help people of all races."

In 1882, Anna died. She had been too shy to travel with her famous husband. But she helped him in everything he did.

Later, Douglass married Helen Pitts, the daughter of an old American family. Helen helped him with his work. When he became ambassador to Haiti, she went with him.

Douglass called his later life the "Golden Years." He spent happy days writing letters and articles at Cedar Hill. In the evenings, friends came to visit. He often played the violin, while Helen played the piano. Sometimes the two danced the Virginia reel. Friends said, "Douglass seems youthful for the first time in his life."

Hundreds of black people wrote to Douglass for advice. They brought their problems to him and called him the "Sage of Anacostia." A sage is a wise man.

Douglass was happy to see young black people growing up to become leaders. Blacks were now citizens. They could vote. Many were getting good schooling. Douglass told them, "Believe in America. Liberty, justice, and fair play will win out in the end."

On February 20, 1895, the Women's Council held

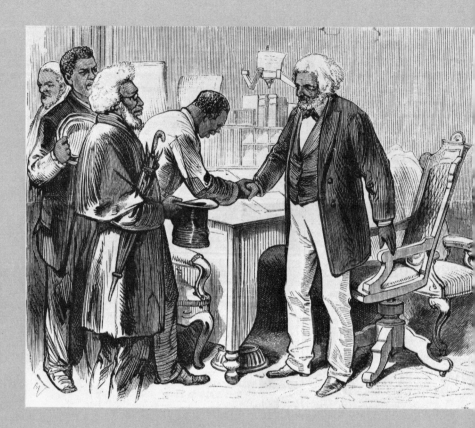

Frederick Douglass accepts the congratulations of his friends on his appointment as marshal of Washington, D.C. In his "golden years," Douglass was honored for the role he played in the struggle to free the slaves and to secure their civil rights.

a meeting in Washington. When Douglass came into the hall, the women all stood and waved white handkerchiefs. "Douglass! Douglass!"

That evening, Douglass was telling Helen about the meeting. Suddenly he sank to his knees and died. He was buried in Rochester, where he had run his Railroad and his *North Star*.

To black people, and to many others too, Douglass had been the North Star, holding out hope of freedom and equality.

Theodore Tilton, a famous poet and editor, wrote a book of poems about Douglass. Tilton said:

> *I knew the noblest giants of my day,*
> *And he was of them.*

HARRIET TUBMAN
About 1821–1913

Iron-willed and courageous, Maryland slave Harriet Tubman was determined to be free. With the help of the Underground Railroad, she made her escape and then returned to the South again and again to lead hundreds of other slaves to freedom. She was a tower of strength to the terrified people she guided through each danger-filled mile of the South to safety in the northern states and Canada. This "Moses of her people," as she came to be called, served as an army scout and as a nurse during the Civil War. But her proudest title of all was "conductor on the Underground Railroad."

Harriet Tubman
Guide to Freedom

by Sam and Beryl Epstein

1. Wanted Dead or Alive

In Maryland, one night in 1852, two armed men galloped along a road. They stopped to nail a sheet of paper to a tree. Large letters on the paper said:

WANTED

DEAD OR ALIVE

HARRIET "MOSES" TUBMAN

$12,000 REWARD

The paper also described Harriet Tubman. She was a black slave about five feet tall. She had scars on her back and a deep scar on her forehead. She was wanted for "stealing" slaves.

"We will never catch her on this road," one of the men said. "The guards at the bridge have the best chance of winning the reward."

"Let's join them," the other man said.

They rode on. The sound of their horses' hooves died away.

The night was silent. Only faint rustlings sounded

in the deep woods on both sides of the road. Suddenly someone began to sing a hymn in a husky voice:

Dark and thorny is the pathway
Where the pilgrim makes his ways;
But beyond this vale of sorrow
Lie the fields of endless days.

The voice sang the song twice. Then a short, stocky black woman stepped out onto the road. She wore an old coat, a long skirt, and a bandanna on her head.

After a few moments a tall black man crept out and joined her.

"Have they gone, Harriet?" he whispered.

"Of course," she snapped at him. "I told you that when I sing that song twice, it means you are safe."

One by one other black people came out of the woods. Six were men; three were women. One carried a sleeping baby.

"Look!" one of the men said. He was the only one in the group who could read. He was pointing to the paper. "It says you are wanted, Harriet. Dead or alive!"

"They have wanted me for a long time," Harriet Tubman said. "But they have not caught me yet."

She reached up and tore down the paper. "Now we can forget it," she said.

"I'm scared, Harriet," a woman said. "They might be waiting for you at the bridge. Then we will all be caught."

Harriet Tubman started to cross the road. "We won't use the bridge," she said. "I know other ways to get over a river. Now come. We have a long way to go before sunup."

They followed her into the woods on the far side of the road. Harriet was their "Moses." Like Moses in the Bible, she led her people toward their "Promised Land." On that night in 1852, she was leading nine more slaves north to freedom.

2. Hired Out

Harriet Tubman was born about 1821. Her father's name was Benjamin Ross. Her mother, also named Harriet, was called Old Rit.

Ben and Old Rit had eleven children. Their home was a one-room cabin on the Maryland plantation of Edward Brodas. Brodas owned them, along with many other slaves.

The cabin floor was packed dirt. Light and air came in only through the door. There were no windows. There was no furniture. Only an iron cooking pot hung over the open fire. The family slept on piles of old rags.

Every morning Ben and Old Rit went out to work for their master. The older children went with them. When Harriet was very small, she stayed behind with the other slave children. They played on the bare earth in front of the row of slave cabins. Their toys were sticks, stones, and chicken feathers.

Sometimes the children helped pick fruit in the master's orchard. Sometimes they helped gather eggs in the hen yard. Then they carried the fruit and eggs up to the "big house." That was what they called the house where the Brodas family lived. All the fine food produced on the plantation went there.

The slaves ate whatever the master gave them. Usually it was cheap salt pork or salt fish, cornmeal mush, or potatoes.

After supper, on warm nights, the slave families sat outside their doorways. Harriet was held on her mother's lap. Often a slave from a nearby plantation joined them. He came silently, in the dark, bringing bits of news.

"The slaves know what is going on before we do," the white people said. "They must have some kind of secret telegraph."

Sometimes an old slave told stories, and Harriet listened. She laughed when the grown-ups laughed. She felt sad when the stories made the grown-ups sigh and shake their heads.

One old man told very sad stories. He told how people had been taken from Africa as prisoners bound in chains. This was before the American colonies had freed themselves from England. In those days Maryland plantations needed as many slaves as they could get. They grew tobacco then for England.

"But now our masters grow pigs and corn," the old man said one night. "They don't need so many slaves anymore. What will become of us?"

"We will be sold down the river," a young man muttered.

Even little Harriet knew what that meant. Slaves sold "down the river" went to cotton, rice or sugar plantations in the Deep South. There, people said, they had to work under a blazing sun until they dropped. Then cruel overseers whipped them to their feet again.

"I will run away if he tries to sell me," another young man said.

"Hush," Old Rit said quickly. It was dangerous to talk of running away. "Master is a good man. He would never sell any of us down the river."

"Then he will hire us out instead," the first young man said. "And that can be just as bad."

"Hiring out" meant sending a slave away to work for someone else. The owner of the slave received the money for the work his slave did.

Old Rit said, "We must put our trust in God. I pray every day that master will let our family stay together."

Other mothers, all up and down the row of cabins, whispered, "Amen."

Then Old Rit began to sing one of her favorite hymns. Harriet sang along with her in her small clear voice. In Old Rit's arms she felt safe and happy.

One day when Harriet was about five years old, the master sent for her.

Edward Brodas was talking to a white woman. The woman stared at Harriet.

"She doesn't look like much," the woman said.

"You said you did not want to pay me much," Edward Brodas answered. "So you will have to take a young slave without any training."

"All right," the woman said. "Get in," she told Harriet. She pointed to a wagon.

Harriet looked at her master. Her knees trembled.

"Do what Miss Susan tells you," he said. He waited until Harriet climbed into the wagon. Then he walked away.

Harriet curled up on the wagon floor. She was trying not to cry, but she was very frightened. She was going to a strange place with a strange woman. She thought she might never see her family again. She had been hired out.

3. The Little Good-for-Nothing

Miss Susan took Harriet into a big house. "Your work is to take care of the baby," Miss Susan said. "But you will have other things to do too. First sweep the floor and dust the furniture."

"Yes, ma'am," Harriet said. But she did not know how to clean polished floors and fine furniture. She had never seen such things before. She left streaks on the floor and dust on the furniture. Miss Susan beat her unmercifully.

Every day Harriet had to rock the baby in her arms for many hours. Sometimes she fell asleep. Miss Susan beat her then too. Finally Miss Susan took Harriet back to Edward Brodas.

"I don't want her in the house," she said.

Edward Brodas soon found new masters for Harriet. They were Mr. and Mrs. Cook, people who had very little money. Mr. Cook trapped muskrats and sold their skins. Mrs. Cook wove cloth. She planned to teach Harriet to help her.

"You will sleep there," she told the little girl. She pointed to the floor near the fireplace.

In the morning Harriet had to clean the fireplace and build a new fire. She had to carry heavy buckets of water from the well and wash dirty pots.

Then Mrs. Cook took her into the weaving room

and shut the door. Harriet felt as if she had been locked in a prison.

"Sit down at the loom," Mrs. Cook said. "And do as I tell you."

Harriet's small fingers got tangled in the yarn. She dropped spools.

"Stupid," Mrs. Cook shouted, and she slapped Harriet's face.

Days went by. Harriet hated the weaving room. She still tangled yarns and dropped spools.

"She can't learn," Mrs. Cook said. "She is too stupid."

"I will put her to work for me," Mr. Cook said. "She can tend my muskrat traps."

Harriet was glad to be out of the house. But tending the traps was hard, lonely work. Every day she had to wade for miles through icy creeks and marshes. She was always cold and wet.

One night she became sick and was burning with fever. There was a pain as sharp as fire in her throat. In the morning she could not stand up. The Cooks thought she was going to die. They let Ben come and take her home.

Old Rit gave Harriet a bitter medicine made from roots and herbs. She told Ben their daughter also needed fresh meat and fish. Ben said he would get them.

He was taking a great risk. A slave who dared to go hunting or fishing might be severely punished. But Ben secretly set snares and caught rabbits. He stole out at night and caught fish.

Slowly Harriet's fever went down. The pain in her throat went away. But her clear voice was gone. From then on her voice was always husky. But she got well.

Edward Brodas wanted to send her back to Mrs. Cook to learn weaving. If Harriet became a good weaver, he could hire her out for more money.

"No," Mrs. Cook said. "I will not keep her. She will never learn anything."

Harriet hoped she would be able to stay at home now. Instead, Brodas hired her out once more as a baby nurse. Again she was shut up in a house that felt like a prison.

One day Harriet saw some cubes of sugar in a bowl. She wanted very much to taste one. She thought her mistress was not looking at her. Harriet reached out her hand.

"Stop!" her mistress shouted. She reached for a whip.

Harriet ran. She raced out of the house and through the yard. She could not go home because she did not know the way. She simply ran until she could not run anymore. Then she hid behind a fence in a field.

There were pigs in the field. That night Harriet

tried to get some of the food that was thrown to the pigs. The big animals pushed her away.

At the end of four days, she was starving. She knew she had to leave the field. She knew there was only one place she could go. She had to return to the house she had run away from.

Harriet's mistress grabbed her the moment she saw her. She held Harriet with one hand and beat her with the other. Time after time the whip lashed down across the little girl's back.

Then the mistress called one of her own slaves. "Take this little good-for-nothing back to Edward Brodas," she said.

That whipping left deep scars on Harriet's back. The scars never disappeared as long as she lived.

4. Learning to Be a Rebel

Edward Brodas decided Harriet would never be a good house servant. He put her to work in the fields. There Harriet proved she could be a good worker. Soon she was doing the job of a grown-up. She plowed with oxen and mules. She harvested corn.

She liked being outdoors all day. She liked being at home with her family at night. But every day Harriet understood better what it meant to be a slave. Every day she hated slavery more.

Nat Turner and his followers. Turner's rebellion resulted in new and stricter rules for slaves.

She was proud when she learned about the black preacher Nat Turner. Turner had led a slave rebellion in Virginia. He and his followers had killed many white slave owners before they were caught and put to death.

"He was a great man," Harriet told her mother one day. She was about fifteen years old then. She already wore the long skirts of a woman.

"He brought us nothing but trouble," Old Rit said. "Nat Turner is the cause of all the new rules."

Harriet knew this was true. One of the new rules for slaves said they could no longer go to church. Their masters were afraid to let them meet there. They were afraid the slaves would plan another revolt behind church doors.

A second new rule said slaves could not talk in the fields, for fear they would talk of revolt. They could not keep silent either. Silent slaves might also be planning a revolution. Slaves had to sing as they worked.

"But Nat Turner was right!" Harriet said. "If slaves do not fight their masters or run away from them, they will never be free."

"It is a sin to talk like that," Old Rit told her. "God made us slaves, and we must accept God's will."

Harriet shook her head stubbornly. "No," she said. "White men made us slaves. And some slaves have already won their freedom. I've heard that all slaves in Mexico are now free."

"Hush!" Old Rit was frightened. "Folks will call you a troublemaker if they hear you talk like that," she said.

Harriet kept quiet then. But she did not change her way of thinking.

One autumn day not long afterward, Harriet and some other slaves were shucking corn in a barn. Suddenly Harriet saw a young slave slip quietly out through the door. He ran across the field and down the road. The overseer saw him too. He started after the slave with a whip in his hand.

The other slaves stood very still. They knew trouble was coming. They wanted to keep out of it. Only Harriet moved. She raced after the overseer. The young slave ran into the village store. The overseer was right behind him. Harriet was right behind the overseer.

"I'll whip you good," the overseer shouted. "That will teach you not to leave your work."

He saw Harriet. "Catch him," he ordered.

The slave made a dash through the door. The overseer spun around to follow him, but Harriet blocked the doorway.

The overseer grabbed a heavy weight from the scales on the counter. He threw it after the running slave. The weight struck Harriet in the forehead. Blood poured from a great gash. She fell backward and lay still.

5. Runaway

Harriet lay unconscious for days in Old Rit's cabin. At last she opened her eyes. She took a little soup and fell asleep again. From then on, very slowly, she got better.

Her wound healed, but it left a big scar on her forehead. And after that, all her life, Harriet had "spells," as she called them. Several times each day she fell into a deep sleep. Sometimes it lasted only a few minutes, sometimes longer. Those spells were a result of the wound.

Edward Brodas tried to sell Harriet.

"I hear she's a troublemaker," some slave buyers said. They would not even look at her.

Those who did look saw the girl fall asleep before their eyes. "She is not worth a penny," they said.

Sometimes Harriet was only pretending to be asleep. The trick always worked. She stayed on at the Brodas plantation. After a time she was strong enough to work again.

Then Edward Brodas died. His son was too young to run the plantation. A manager ran it for him. The manager hired out all the slaves he did not need. He hired Ben Ross out to John Stewart, a lumber merchant. He hired Harriet out to the same man.

Ben Ross was put in charge of a gang of slave lumbermen. Harriet asked Stewart to let her work in the forest with her father. Stewart was a kind master. He agreed.

Ben was proud of his daughter. "You can cut down a tree as fast as any man in the gang," he said. "You can pick up logs that some of my men can't lift."

One day Stewart told Harriet she could "hire her time." This meant she could go to work for anyone who wanted to pay her. She had to give Stewart part of her wages, but she could still save a little every week.

For the first time in her life, Harriet had some money. Perhaps that is why John Tubman married her when she was about 24 years old.

John Tubman had been born free, because his slave parents had been set free by their master. He was a happy-go-lucky young man who sang and joked all day long.

Harriet was proud to be his wife. She did not complain because he earned very little. She was glad to share her own money with him. For a time she was happy. She seemed to forget her old ideas about rebellion and running away.

Suddenly young Brodas died. Slave buyers began to arrive at the plantation. Soon two of Harriet's sisters were sold. Harriet heard that she and her brothers would be sold too.

"I have a friend who will help us run away," she told her husband. "We must go quickly."

Her friend was a white woman who always spoke to Harriet when they passed on the road. Once the woman had asked about the scar on Harriet's forehead. Harriet told her about the blow that had almost killed her. "If you ever need help, Harriet," the kind woman had told her, "you must be sure to come to me."

Harriet had understood. She realized that the kind woman must be part of the Underground Railroad. This was a group of people who helped slaves escape to the North. The home of each member of the group was a "station" on the "railroad." Slaves were sent secretly from one station to the next. Some members acted as "conductors" to help slaves on their way.

The Underground Railroad took slaves into Pennsylvania and into other northern states. There they were free. Slavery was against the law in those states.

"Let's go north together, John," Harriet begged her husband.

John laughed at her. He did not want to leave his lazy life in Maryland. He did not want Harriet to go either.

"You will get one of your spells on the road," he said. "Then you would surely be caught."

"You could help me," Harriet said. "We must take the chance!"

"I won't go," John said. "And if you try to go, I'll tell your master. He will send men and dogs after you."

Harriet hated to believe that her own husband would betray her. But she could see that he meant what he said. She let him think she had given up the plan.

Later she slipped out and found three of her brothers.

"Let's run away together," she said.

At first they agreed. Then they became frightened and would not go. They tried to keep Harriet from going too.

But Harriet had made up her mind. She had already paid a secret visit to her white friend. The woman had told her how to find the first Underground Railroad station on her way.

"Show this paper to the woman at that house," Harriet's friend had said.

She gave Harriet a paper with two names written on it. Harriet hid the tiny scrap of paper. She could take nothing else with her except a little food tucked in her pocket.

She wanted to say good-bye to Old Rit and Ben. But she did not dare. They might not be able to keep her secret. Instead, she went up to the big Brodas house where her sister Mary worked.

Mary saw her and came out of the kitchen. Just then they both saw the plantation manager riding toward them. Harriet knew Mary would be in trouble if he caught them together. She walked quickly away. As she left, she sang:

> *I'm sorry I'm going to leave you,*
> *Farewell, oh, farewell.*
> *I'll meet you in the morning*
> *Safe in the promised land.*

"Mary will remember the song when she hears I am gone," Harriet told herself. "She will understand what it means."

That night Harriet waited until John was asleep. Then she crept out of the cabin and into the woods. She looked up at the dark sky, twinkling with stars.

"There is the North Star," she told herself. "If I follow it long enough, it will lead me to freedom."

6. The Underground Railroad to Freedom

Harriet walked all that night. At dawn she went to sleep in a burrow deep in the underbrush.

Late in the afternoon she set out again. Whenever she came to a road, she looked carefully before darting across it. She climbed hills and struggled through swamps. Sometimes she waded a mile or two along a riverbed. She knew bloodhounds could not follow her trail through water.

Finally Harriet had to walk openly along the road. It was the only way she could look for the Underground Railroad station. She pulled her bandanna down over the deep scar on her forehead. She bent her head and shuffled along like an old woman.

"Please, God, let me not have one of my spells out here," she prayed.

Finally she saw a house like the one her friend had told her to look for. A woman was feeding hens in the yard.

Harriet held out her scrap of paper. "Do you know these two names?" she asked.

The woman nodded. Quickly she handed Harriet a broom. "Sweep the yard," she told her. "Then anyone who comes along will think you are a servant."

When the woman's husband came home, he called Harriet into the house. "The patrol is watching our road," he said. "I will take you the next few miles hidden in our wagon."

They gave Harriet some food. They covered her with blankets. The wagon did not stop until it was far from the house. There the man helped Harriet out.

"God keep you safe," he said.

"God bless you for your help," Harriet answered. Then once more she walked off alone through the night.

Days went by. Harriet hid during daylight hours.

She went on again as soon as darkness fell. Once a poor black family gave her a little food. She found the second Underground Railroad station with no trouble. A conductor for the Railroad led her into busy Wilmington, Delaware, a dangerous place for runaway slaves.

The conductor took her to a dark house and rapped softly on the door. An upstairs window opened. A man peered out.

"I have a shipment for you," the conductor said. "One bale of cotton."

"I was expecting the shipment," the man in the window said. "I will open the door for thee, friend."

He was Thomas Garrett, a Quaker. Harriet knew he had been put in jail for helping runaway slaves. But he was still willing to help people who were trying to escape from slavery.

Harriet stayed at the Garrett house for two days. Finally a Quaker woman took her out of the city in her wagon.

"Remember, Harriet," the woman said. "If we are stopped, I will say that thee is my servant."

They were not stopped. When the city was far behind them, Harriet left the wagon for the last stretch of her journey.

"That path will lead thee to the border of Pennsylvania," the woman told her. "A wooden signpost marks the border. But take care. Patrollers are often on watch there."

Harriet ran along the path. When she finally saw the signpost she stopped. She looked around. There was no one in sight. Quickly she ran across the boundary.

The rising sun spread a golden light over everything. Harriet stood in the glow and whispered, "I'm free! I'm free!"

7. Underground Railroad Conductor

Harriet walked on through Pennsylvania until she reached Philadelphia. There she found a job and went to work. She moved about from job to job whenever she liked. It was her way of enjoying her new freedom.

But she worried about her family. She wanted to know what was happening back in Maryland. Finally she got news through a new friend, William Still. He was a black member of the Philadelphia Vigilance Committee. This was a group of people who helped runaway slaves. Its office was a station of the Underground Railroad.

"Your sister Mary and her children are going to be sold," William Still told Harriet. "They must be rescued. Her husband can take them as far as Baltimore. We will send someone to lead them on from there."

"I will go," Harriet said. "I know the way. I know where the Underground Railroad stations are."

"But you must not return to the South," William Still said. "You might be arrested and sent back to your master."

"I will be careful," Harriet promised. "And I have bought a pistol. If I am arrested, I will kill myself."

Soon Harriet returned with Mary and her family.

"Now I know what I want to do with my life," she told Still. "I want to go South as often as I can, and free more of my people."

Then William Still told her about the new Fugitive Slave Law. It said that a runaway slave could now be arrested anywhere, even in the North.

"Is there no place where slaves can be safe?" Harriet asked.

"They are safe in Canada, hundreds of miles to the north," Still answered. "The laws of Canada protect runaway slaves."

"From now on I will take slaves there," Harriet said.

She set to work to earn some money. Then she went south to Maryland to "steal" more slaves.

First she rescued one of her brothers and two other men. Then on her next trip she took half a dozen slaves North. On the trip after that, she ran off with eleven slaves.

Once she tried to take her husband north. John Tubman refused to go. He said Harriet had left him forever. He had married another woman.

Harriet took the runaways to the little town of St. Catherines in Canada. She stayed with them until they were settled. She helped them find places to live. She found jobs for them. She made a home for herself in St. Catherines too. But she never stayed there very long. Each time she earned some money, she set off to rescue more men and women.

People who made the trip north with Harriet had to be strong. Only strong men and women could walk for miles, night after night. They also had to be brave.

Sometimes a slave became frightened along the way. He said he was afraid to go on. He wanted to turn back. Then Harriet had to be firm.

"No," she always said. "You already know too much about the Underground Railroad. You might tell what you know if your master beat you hard enough. Then we would all be in danger."

If the frightened runaway still said he wanted to go back, Harriet took out her pistol. "Either you come with us," she told the runaway, "or you will die here."

She never had to use the gun. Soon even the most frightened men followed her without question.

They did not try to turn back even when she had one of her spells. They waited until she woke up.

Harriet led to freedom many people she did not know. They were people who had heard of her and asked for her help. She also saved all her own brothers and sisters, except the two who had been sold. Then she saved her mother and father.

She had made many trips south without trying to rescue her parents. She thought they were too old for the long journey. Then she heard that her father might be sent to jail for helping a runaway slave. She started south again immediately.

Runaway slaves endured danger and hardship on the trip north by Underground Railroad.

Before she reached her parents' cabin, she stopped at the house of a friend.

"My folks are too old to walk," she told him. "But I must take them north. I need a horse and something for them to ride in."

"You may have my horse," the friend said quickly. "But my wagon is useless."

"Then I will have to make a carriage for them," Harriet said.

Her friend helped her. Somewhere they found an old pair of light wheels. They found enough planks to make a seat and a footrest. Soon the simple "carriage" was finished.

Harriet went to the cabin of her parents after dark. Old Rit cried for joy at the sight of her.

"You're going to ride to freedom," Harriet said.

All through the night she guided the creaking carriage along the rutted roads. Then at daybreak they reached a small town. Harriet left her parents for a few minutes.

"Here are your train tickets," she said when she came back. "And here are false passes for you. The passes say your master gives you permission to visit your grandchildren in Wilmington. When you get to Wilmington, you must go to the house of Thomas Garrett. He is my good friend. He will take care of you until I arrive."

Old Rit grabbed Harriet's hand. "But aren't you coming with us?" she asked.

Harriet smiled. She took a sheet of paper out of her old bag. It was a reward poster with her picture on it.

"Papers like this are on the walls of every station from here to Wilmington," she said. "If I got on that train, I would be arrested right away."

A train whistle sounded in the distance. Harriet hugged her father and mother. "The station is around the corner," she said. "Just get on the train when it comes. And don't worry about me. I will see you in Wilmington. From there we will travel to Canada."

8. Tricks and Disguises

Harriet Tubman had become famous. For a long time almost nobody knew her by her real name. People knew her only as "Moses." Black people gave her that name because she had led so many of them out of slavery. Even her white friends in the North used it. They always called her Moses in public.

"It is safer for you," they told her. "A woman named Harriet Tubman is listed among the runaways from Maryland. Anyone who learns your real name could have you arrested. But no slave owner has claimed that someone named Moses belongs to him."

Moses often spoke at abolitionist meetings in Boston and other cities. Abolitionists were people who believed slavery should be abolished—done away with.

Harriet told them how slaves were treated by their owners. She told them how the Underground Railroad carried slaves to freedom. The abolitionists clapped and cheered when she finished. Then they collected money to help more runaways.

Slave owners in the South had thought at first that Moses was a man.

"That devil has cost us thousands of dollars in lost slaves," they said. "If we only knew who he is, and what he looks like, we could catch him."

Then they had discovered who Moses was. Immediately they had printed the posters that told what Harriet looked like. They also offered huge rewards for the capture of Harriet "Moses" Tubman.

"Now we will catch that devil!" they said. "Hundreds of people will be looking for her. They will all want to win the reward money."

But Harriet was too clever for her enemies. She used all sorts of tricks to fool them. She usually started her trips north on a Saturday night.

"By the time your masters miss you, it will be Sunday," she told the runaways. "And they will not be able to organize a search patrol until Monday. That gives us a head start of two whole days."

Now that she was known to be a woman, Harriet sometimes dressed as a man. And she often dressed and walked like a very old "granny."

One day she was near the Brodas plantation. She was pretending to be an old woman on her way to market. She carried two chickens tied together by their legs.

Suddenly she saw the plantation manager riding toward her on his horse. Quickly she untied the chickens. They flapped away into a field, squawking and fluttering. Harriet ran after them waving her hands.

The manager roared with laughter. "Run, granny!" he shouted. "Catch 'em, granny!" He watched until Harriet was out of sight. He never guessed that he was watching the famous Moses—the runaway slave from his own plantation.

Once Harriet used her granny disguise to save a runaway slave from being sent back south. The slave had been captured in Troy, New York. He was being held prisoner in a government building. He was handcuffed. Police and other officers guarded him night and day. Soon his master arrived to take him back to Virginia.

Harriet heard the news. So did hundreds of abolitionists in the town. They all gathered outside the building.

Other people gathered there too. They were glad the runaway had been captured. They wanted him to be sent back to slavery. "Send him back!" they shouted.

"Free him! Free him!" the abolitionists shouted.

Finally the runaway slave appeared. Guards stood all around him. He still wore handcuffs.

Harriet pushed through the crowd until she was near him. She was bent far over like a little old woman.

"Stand back, granny," a policeman said. "You'll be hurt."

Harriet pretended not to hear. All around her, voices were still shouting.

"Free him!"

"Send him back!"

Harriet edged closer and closer to the runaway. Suddenly she grabbed him. She held him in her strong arms and started to drag him away from his guards.

"Help us get to the river," she called. "Free him!"

Abolitionists cleared a path for her. They blocked the guards who tried to follow Harriet. Other people fought the abolitionists and tried to recapture the runaway. Blows rained down on Harriet from fists and clubs. Hands pulled at her clothes. Her skirt was ripped to shreds.

Nothing stopped her. Somehow she managed to get him all the way to the river. There an abolitionist waited in a small boat. A moment later the runaway was being rowed toward safety. Abolitionists on the other side of the river protected him. With their help he reached Canada safely.

Harriet had to hide from the police. Friends sheltered her in their homes for days. Finally she was able to slip away. Not long afterward she was on her way south again—to steal more slaves.

9. General Tubman

"There is only one way to free all slaves," Harriet Tubman often told her abolitionist friends. "We must make war against the slave owners and win."

Not all abolitionists agreed with her. Some thought they could abolish slavery by law. But John Brown, a great abolitionist leader, thought as Harriet did. He planned a rebellion against slave owners. He asked Harriet to help him. He called her "General" Tubman.

"I will recruit men for your army," Harriet promised.

Then she became sick. She was in bed for weeks. John Brown had to start his rebellion without Harriet and her recruits. He made his first attack at Harpers

John Brown and his men met disaster at Harpers Ferry.

Ferry in West Virginia. In two days he was defeated. Some of his men died during the fighting. John Brown and others were hanged.

Harriet was sad over the death of her friend.

"But there will be another war to free the slaves someday," she said. "And that one will end in victory."

By then Harriet had a little house of her own in Auburn, New York. Her mother and father lived there with her. Her abolitionist friends helped protect them all from slave catchers.

Harriet still went south as often as she could to steal more slaves. Altogether she rescued more than

200 men, women, and children. She made her last trip in November 1860. In that same month Abraham Lincoln was elected president. A few months later the Civil War broke out. It was the war that Harriet believed would free the slaves.

Northern army leaders sent for Harriet.

"We need your help," one of them said. "But we will not be able to pay you."

"Do you think I was paid for working with the Underground Railroad?" Harriet asked in surprise. "I have always looked after myself. I still can. Now what do you want me to do?"

They sent her first to Beaufort, South Carolina. That town was held by Yankee soldiers from the North. Runaway slaves poured into Beaufort every day. Many were sick or hurt. All were frightened.

"These people do not trust us, Harriet," General David Hunter said. "Their masters always told them that Yankees are cruel to Negroes. But they will trust you. Do what you can for them."

Every day Harriet worked in a hospital set up for the black people.

Soon they, too, began to call Harriet their Moses. They asked for her advice. She helped them learn to live as free men. When President Lincoln decided to take black men into the Northern army, many of the men at Beaufort were ready to go.

Harriet next served as a scout. With nine men to help her, she explored the countryside at night. She looked for enemy fortifications. She looked for weak spots in the enemy's defenses. Yankee officers used her information to help plan their attacks.

Once Harriet and her men explored the Combahee River. Then they took part in a big raid up that river. The raiding troops were black. They traveled in three gunboats. Harriet rode in the first boat.

"Stop here," she ordered near a bend in the river. "There is an enemy post just around the bend."

Soldiers went ashore. They crept around behind the enemy. They captured the post without firing a shot.

The gunboats moved upstream again. Harriet gave another order.

"Go slowly," she said. "There are enemy mines in the river here."

Harriet and her men pointed out where the mines were hidden. The boats passed them without trouble.

During this same raid, the black soldiers destroyed large stores of cotton. The enemy would have sold that cotton to buy guns and ammunition. The soldiers also freed more than 700 slaves and brought them to safety.

Later Harriet served as a nurse in a Virginia hospital. She did that work, too, without pay. She was still working there when the war ended in April 1865.

Harriet Tubman's courage and her knowledge of the countryside made her a valuable army scout.

Harriet was weary after the long years of war. She had very little money. But she was happy. Slavery had been abolished. All blacks were now free. She was ready to go home. Harriet hoped to spend the rest of her life in peace.

An army officer gave Harriet a pass for the railroad. It said she could travel at half fare because she was a nurse. As soon as she could she got on a train heading north.

The train conductor spoke to her as soon as she took her seat. "You can't sit there," he said.

Harriet showed him her pass. He brushed it aside. "We don't allow Negroes in this car," he said. "Ride in the baggage car."

"But I am free," Harriet said. "I have a right to ride in this car—as much right as anyone."

The conductor called two other men. "Get her out of here," he said.

Together they dragged Harriet out of the car. They pulled her to the baggage car and shoved her in. Then they shut the door.

When Harriet reached Auburn, there were bruises all over her body. Her friends thought she had been hurt during the war.

Harriet shook her head. "I went all through the war without a scratch," she told them. "I was hurt because I tried to ride in a car with white folks."

The journey home had taught her a sad lesson. She knew now that even free blacks did not share all the rights of other Americans. She knew that her people still needed help.

10. "Oh, Go Down, Moses"

Harriet found her parents safe. Friends had looked after them while she was gone.

"Now I will take care of you," she said.

Once more she went to work in the fields. She raised vegetables and sold them from house to house.

Soon other black people came to her home. Some were sick; some were hungry. Harriet took them all in. Somehow she managed to help them all.

One sick man who came to her door was a black man who had fought in the Civil War. His name was Nelson Davis. Harriet nursed him. After a time she and Nelson Davis were married. Almost everyone in Auburn came to the wedding.

The only money Harriet ever received from the government came to her through Nelson Davis. When he died, she was given a pension of $8 a month. This was the sum the government paid to the widow of a soldier. Later the sum was raised to $20 a month.

With this money and with gifts from her friends, Harriet could now do what she had planned for a long time. She turned her house into a real home for poor and sick blacks. She called it the "John Brown Home" in honor of the famous abolitionist fighter.

Many important people traveled to Auburn to visit Harriet when she was an old woman. Some of them had read a book by Sarah Bradford, an Auburn schoolteacher. The book was called *Harriet Tubman: The Moses of Her People*. It told the exciting story of Harriet's life. The visitors wanted to pay their respects to the Moses of the Underground Railroad.

Harriet was famous even in Europe. Once she received a letter from Queen Victoria of England. The queen had ruled England for 50 years. The English were planning to celebrate her anniversary. The queen invited Harriet to the celebration.

Harriet could not afford the trip to England. But she always kept that letter.

Harriet was very often asked to make speeches in Boston and other cities. One group that invited her was trying to win the right for women to vote. In those days only men could vote. Harriet thought that everyone—men and women, black and white—should have the same rights. She was glad to accept their invitation to speak.

Harriet always appeared on a platform in neat, old-fashioned clothes. Once in a while she fell asleep for a minute or two while she was waiting to speak.

Everyone knew about her spells. They knew she would soon wake up again and be ready to talk.

Sometimes she talked about her work in the war. But most people wanted to hear about the Underground Railroad. She told about her narrow escapes. She told about using songs as signals to the runaways. She told how slaves sang out their joy when they reached Canada.

"Sing for us, Harriet," people often said.

The song they most wanted to hear was one that seemed to belong to Harriet. She had sung it often as a signal to slaves. Now she sang it for her friends:

> *Oh, go down, Moses,*
> *Way down into Egypt's land,*
> *Tell old Pharaoh,*
> *Let my people go.*

Harriet died in 1913. She was over 90 years old. After her death her friends continued to run her home for poor and sick blacks. But they gave it a new name. They called it the "Harriet Tubman Home."

Her friends also remembered something Harriet had often said. They put the words on a bronze tablet set up in her honor in Auburn. The words are:

"On my Underground Railroad I never ran my train off the track. And I never lost a passenger."

BOOKER T. WASHINGTON
1856–1915

Tuskegee's beloved "Mr. B.T." was determined to teach his students to take their place in a free society. "We train your hands, head, and heart," he told them. "And we help you in these ways that you, in turn, may help others." Mr. B.T. exemplified this idea in his own life. Born in slavery, he had undergone terrible hardship in order to go to school. Now at Tuskegee, brick by brick, he was building a school and, at the same time, helping his people to build new lives free from the burden of the long, grinding years of slavery.

Booker T. Washington

Leader of His People

by Lillie Patterson

1. A Slave Boy Called Booker

The summer sun woke Booker. It streamed into the one-room slave cabin.

Seven-year-old Booker blinked sleep from his eyes. Then he shook his sleeping brother. "Wake up, John! Sun's high!" The boys slept on the floor on a pallet made of grain sacks. Baby sister Amanda, called Mandy, slept on another pallet.

There was almost no furniture in the cabin. The floor was the bare earth. A rough wooden table stood against one wall. Two benches were also in the room. But there was no real bed, no stove. Beside a big stone fireplace hung iron pots and kettles. Booker's mother was the plantation cook.

The door opened. Booker jumped across the potato hole in the middle of the floor. Sweet potatoes were stored in the hole in winter months. "Good morning, ma!" Booker called.

"Good morning, son." Booker's mother kissed his light brown face, his wide forehead. "You're growing like a weed."

Her name was Jane. Most slaves had only one name.

"Did you bring our Sunday treat, ma?"

"Two treats!" Jane reached into a basket. "Here's the first one."

"No!" Booker backed away, his eyes wide with horror. "Not a new shirt, ma."

"I know it's rough, Booker. But in a few weeks it will be as soft as one made of cotton."

They lived in Franklin County, Virginia. There, slave clothes were made from flax. Slave boys wore only a shirt that came down to their knees. Sharp bits of flax pricked like needles.

"My poor skin," Booker moaned.

Eleven-year-old John walked over to his mother. "I'll wear the shirt until it's soft," he said.

The second Sunday treat was molasses. Other times they ate only corn bread and fat pork. Booker tipped his tin plate until the sweet molasses ran all over it. "This always makes it seem more," he said.

Booker's owner was James Burroughs. It was 1863. The Civil War was being fought between the North and the South. Abraham Lincoln was president.

Booker helped Mrs. Burroughs in the house and yards. One day she said, "You must walk with my daughters to school and carry their books."

"Yes, ma'am." Booker was always happy out of doors.

They reached the school. Booker peeked into the sunny room. The boys and girls were reading.

The slave cabin in Franklin County, Virginia, where Booker T. Washington was born

"Going to school must be heaven," the slave boy whispered.

That night he said, "I want to learn to read, ma."

"I know, Booker. Every night I pray for freedom. I hope your pa is free now." Jane's husband, Washington Ferguson, was stepfather to Booker and John. He had run away from his owner.

"Why can't slaves go to school?" Booker asked.

"Hush! It's against the law. You keep hoping, child. I'll keep praying."

"I will, ma. And when I learn, I'll teach all the slaves in the world to read."

2. Songs of Freedom

Months passed. The Civil War went on. The Burroughs family became poorer and poorer.

Booker had to do more and more of the work. He did it gladly. The slaves felt sorry for their owners. Each week now Booker took the corn to the mill to be ground. He enjoyed listening to the slaves he met there. They always shared the latest news.

Not one of the slaves could read. Yet they often knew of many happenings long before their owners. Secrets were passed from kitchen to kitchen, from field to field. Slaves called their news system the "grapevine telegraph."

Each day after 1864 news became more exciting. The grapevine telegraph buzzed night and day. "Mr. Lincoln's army is winning! The war will soon be over! All slaves will be free!"

Slaves couldn't stop singing. They made up songs about the day of "jubilo." That was the joyful day they would be free. "Freedom was in the air, and had been for many months," Booker remembered later.

One spring day in 1865, Mrs. Burroughs sent for her slaves.

They came running. The Burroughs family stood on the porch of their home. All of them were crying.

A man in uniform stepped forward. He told them that the war was over and that slavery was ended in the United States. Then he read a long paper to the slaves. "This is the Emancipation Proclamation," he explained. "It says that you are free."

"Free at last!" A joyful shout rang over the plantation.

Some slaves began to sing. Others started to pray.

Jane dropped to her knees. Tears ran down her cheeks. She gathered Booker, John, and Mandy in her arms. Then she looked up into the bright blue sky. "Thank you, Lord. My prayers are answered."

The freed slaves wandered about aimlessly. They had no food, no homes, no jobs. What would become of them?

Booker's family was lucky. One morning John called, "Booker! Look what's in front of our cabin."

"A donkey," Booker cried.

A soldier had brought the donkey, a cart, and some wonderful news. Booker's stepfather had followed Northern soldiers to West Virginia. Now he wanted his family to come to the town of Malden.

Mrs. Burroughs gave them some food and pots and pans. "Please send word back to me," she said. Jane and Mrs. Burroughs were both crying.

"I'll write," Booker promised. "I'll write as soon as I go to school."

Jane and Mandy rode in the cart. Booker and John walked behind, kicking the dirt happily with their bare feet. None of them had ever been away from Franklin County. None of them could read a word. Yet they bravely set out on a 200-mile trip.

For it was 1865, the magical year of jubilo.

3. A New Home

The trip took many weeks. The family went mile after mile over mountains. Kind strangers helped them to find the right roads. They cooked their meals over campfires. At night they slept under the stars.

Finally they reached Malden. How happy Ferguson was to see them! "The cabin is not much," he said. "But it's our home."

He was right. The cabin was no better than the one they left behind. "I'll fix it up," John promised. "I'll build a kitchen and some tables and benches."

Booker's eyes gleamed with excitement. "Where is the school, pa? Can I start tomorrow?"

"School?" Ferguson frowned. "There's no school here. Besides, you boys must start to work tomorrow."

Booker's high hopes fell. He was too disappointed to say another word.

Jane asked, "Where will they work? Booker is only nine."

"They will work in the salt mines," Ferguson said.

Booker shivered at the sound of the words. He had been so sure that freedom would mean learning to read.

The salt mines were wells dug deep into the earth. Salt water was pumped up from them. When the water was boiled away, wet salt was left. The salt was then dried. Both Booker and John became packers. They beat the salt down into big barrels. The work was hard, even for grown men.

One day as Booker walked home he saw an amazing sight. A strange black man sat on a barrel. Other blacks stood around, listening. The stranger was reading a newspaper to them.

"He is reading!" Booker cried. "He is a Negro and he's reading. If he can do it, so will I."

But there was nothing for Booker to read. There was not even a torn page from a magazine to be found.

Then Booker saw that each salt barrel was marked with a number. He began to read by learning these numbers.

One evening his mother said, "I have a big surprise for you." She gave him a gift.

"A book!" Booker held it gently.

"It's a Webster's Blue-Backed Speller," Jane said. "I saved a little each week to buy it."

Each night after that Booker went to sleep over his book. He studied it very hard until he learned the alphabet. Soon he could read a few words.

Then an exciting thing happened. A school opened in Malden. Booker was overjoyed. "Please let me go," he begged his stepfather.

Ferguson explained, "We are poor. We get very little money for our work. Everyone must work if we are to eat."

Booker's chin trembled. But he was stubborn. "I *am* going to school," he told himself. Each day he begged. So did his mother.

At last Ferguson said, "You can go. But you will have to work before and after school."

"Oh, I will!" Booker promised. "I'll do anything to go to school."

Booker's real day of jubilo had come.

4. New Names—New Hope

It was Booker's first day in school. "What is your name?" the teacher asked.

"Booker, sir."

"Booker, *what?*"

"Oh, dear," Booker thought. "I need a last name. Which shall I choose?" Then he remembered one very famous name.

"Washington!" he answered. "Booker Washington, sir."

That day went well. So did all the days during the next months. He was always up before daylight. There was a two-mile walk to work. He packed salt, then ran to school, then hurried back to work.

But he was a happy schoolboy with a fine new name. He had a new brother, too. Jane adopted an orphan boy named James. John, Mandy, and James all added Booker's last name to their own.

Booker did not go to school long. His stepfather made him leave school to work in the coal mines.

How Booker hated the work under the ground! He still dreamed about going to school. One day he heard two miners talking about a new school.

"Are you sure it's for Negro boys?" the first asked.

"That's right," the other answered. "It's for poor Negro students."

"And what's the name of this school?"

Booker thought he would burst with excitement as he waited. Then the answer came over the coal dust.

"Hampton."

"I'm going to that school," Booker promised himself. "I don't know how I'll get there. But I'm going."

Not long after that, Booker got another job. Mrs. Ruffner was the wife of the owner of the mines. She needed help. Booker knew she was hard to please.

Mrs. Ruffner promised, "If you please me, I will lend you my books."

Booker did please her. Mrs. Ruffner taught him how to take pride in his work. And she let him go to school part of the time.

When Booker was sixteen, he decided to go to find Hampton. He bought a cheap bag. His mother and John saved a little money to buy him some clothes.

Before Booker left home his mother told him something special. She had named him Booker Taliaferro when he was born. So his name became Booker Taliaferro Washington.

Booker started out by horse-drawn stagecoach. Later he took the train. When his money gave out, he started to walk. Finally he reached Richmond, Virginia. Now what would he do next? After a while, he found a high wooden sidewalk and went to sleep under it. The next day he got a job loading iron onto a ship. Each night he slept outdoors so he could save money for his trip.

Autumn was Booker's favorite season. It was autumn when he reached Hampton. How beautiful the campus looked! Trees were bright with red and orange and yellow. Among them stood a tall brick building. Boats sailed upon the blue water nearby.

Later Booker said, "I felt that I had reached the promised land."

5. The Student

"I am Miss Mary Mackie, the head teacher."

Booker faced the white teacher. He was ragged and dirty from his long trip. "Please," he begged. "Please let me stay here and go to school."

Miss Mackie only said, "The next room needs sweeping. Take the broom and sweep it."

This was his test. "How glad I am that I worked for Mrs. Ruffner!" Booker thought.

Booker gladly swept the whole room once, twice, three times. Then he dusted everything in it four times. He washed the woodwork. He shined the doorknobs.

Miss Mackie returned. She rubbed a snowy white handkerchief over tables and benches. Booker held his breath. But not a speck of dust was anywhere. Miss Mackie smiled and said, "I guess you will do to enter this school."

Booker's heart leaped with joy. "I'll make good," he promised.

Miss Mackie gave Booker a job as school janitor. He made the fires each morning before school. He cleaned the rooms each afternoon. No work was too hard. John sent Booker a few dollars whenever he could.

Booker liked all of his teachers. Hampton teachers

were from rich white families. They were spending their lives teaching black people.

Best of all Booker liked the principal, Samuel Chapman Armstrong. Armstrong was tall and handsome with flashing eyes. He had joined the Northern army during the Civil War. He was then a young man just out of college. He became interested in blacks: "I see only the four million slaves, and for them I fight."

After the war General Armstrong said, "The freed slaves need schools." His friends helped him buy a plantation in Hampton, Virginia. In 1868 he opened Hampton Institute there. The school trained teachers. It also taught useful trades, such as carpentry.

"The general is wonderful," Booker said. "I am going to be like him."

Miss Nathalie Lord taught Booker reading. One day she told him, "You have a fine voice. You could become a great speaker. I will use my spare hours to teach you." She taught Booker how to stand and how to breathe. She showed him how to use his hands and his body when he spoke.

Booker was very shy at first.

"Hold a pencil in your hand," Miss Lord said.

This worked. After that, Booker always held a pencil when he gave a speech.

Two years soon passed. Booker went home for the

summer. His family had saved the money to send for him. How happy Jane was to see her son again!

But a sad thing happened. Jane died soon after Booker got home. Booker was shocked. "I wanted to do so much for ma," he told John.

"You can finish school," John said. "That's what she wanted."

"I will!" Booker promised. "And I will send you and James and Mandy to Hampton. Then ma's wish will really come true."

Booker finished Hampton in 1875. General Armstrong said, "Help your people by giving them what has been given to you."

6. Teacher and Indian Chief

Booker went back home to teach in Malden. He was now called Professor Washington.

His day began at eight o'clock. He taught more than eighty students in day school. Then he worked on until ten at night, for he had opened a night school. He taught two Sunday schools too. "I taught anyone who wanted to learn anything that I could teach him," Washington said later.

He also gave special lessons to students who wanted to go to Hampton. John got very special teaching. Soon Booker sent his faithful brother to Hampton.

Booker T. Washington. The young teacher wanted to help other blacks get the kind of education he had received at Hampton.

After three years Washington went to school again. He studied in Washington, D.C., the nation's capital.

"You should study law," some friends said.

"You should go into politics," said others.

Washington began to study law. But he soon forgot both law and politics, for an exciting letter came from General Armstrong.

"I need you," he wrote. "We are beginning an experiment for the United States government. I want to prove that Indians, too, can be educated."

At that time most people said that Indians were too wild to be taught.

Washington returned to Hampton. "I will put the Indians in your care," General Armstrong said. "If we can teach the Indians, then the government might build schools for them."

Soon nearly a hundred young Indians arrived from the West. Washington smiled and said, "Greetings!"

Loud grunts came from the Indians. They could not speak a word of English. Their eyes were angry. They did not want to change their ways of living.

Washington knew how the Indians felt. They were a proud people. Now they would have to give up many old customs. They would have to dress as other students.

"How can I make friends with them?" Washington thought.

He found the answer. He used his big smile and his friendly handshake. He was kind and understanding. "There are many ways of showing brotherhood," he said.

Washington told the students, "We can learn from the Indians." There was one custom the whole school liked. Indians wore soft moccasins on their feet. Soon everyone on the campus gave up shoes for the comfortable moccasins.

The Indians lived in a new building. The students named it the "Wigwam." Washington lived with them as their "housefather." Everyone called him

"Chief." As he taught the Indians to speak English, he won their friendship. Soon he began teaching them other things. Before the end of that year the Indians looked to Washington as their leader. "You really are our chief," they said.

The experiment was a big success. The president and Congress praised it. Hundreds of Indians came to Hampton to study. Later the government opened a special school for Indians.

Washington had done a great thing for the Indians, and for America.

"And I learned, too," Washington said. "I must not think only of helping the Negroes. I must try to help all people."

7. The New School

Now came the biggest surprise of all.

One evening in May 1881, General Armstrong read a letter to his students. It came from Tuskegee, Alabama, a small town in the Deep South.

The letter was from a group of Tuskegee men. One was a white banker, who had once owned slaves. Another was a black shoemaker, who had once been a slave. "Our state has given money to start a school for Negroes," they said. "Please send one of your teachers to be principal."

The next day Armstrong sent for Washington. "I believe you are the person to send. Will you go?"

"I am very willing to try, General Armstrong."

They wrote to Tuskegee. The answer came, "Booker T. Washington will suit us. Send him at once."

What an honor for a young man only 25 years old!

Washington arrived in Tuskegee that June. The town had been named for an Indian chief. Washington could not guess that he, a black man, would make it famous.

"Where's the schoolhouse?" he asked.

There was no schoolhouse. There were no students. "How can I start a school with nothing?" Washington wondered. But he did not give up. "I will visit Negro families," he said. "Then I will know the kind of school they need."

Washington traveled the dusty roads to tell the people about the new school. He slept in the tumble-down cabins. He ate the corn bread and pork which was still the main food. How poor the Negroes were! They had to share their crops with white landlords.

"My people are free," Washington said sadly. "But they have to be taught how to live in freedom."

Where could he begin? Washington formed his idea of education. "Leadership consists in finding folk where they are and guiding them to where they ought to be."

He said, "Negroes need more than book learning just now. I will teach them better ways of farming and useful trades. Then they can earn more money. I will show them how to plant vegetables and eat healthier meals. I will help them save money to buy land and build homes. Then their everyday lives will be happier."

Washington borrowed an old church building. And on the Fourth of July, 1881, he opened his school. There were 30 students. Many were grown men and women.

The school became known as Tuskegee Normal and Industrial Institute. "Normal" meant that it trained teachers. "Industrial" meant that it taught students useful trades, or industries.

The beginning was not easy. There were few books and almost no furniture. When it rained the water came through holes in the roof. Students would run to hold an umbrella over their teacher. There seemed never to be enough money.

"Nothing will stop our school from growing," Washington told his students. "We will use what we have and work to get more."

New students came, begging to stay. Washington could never send them away. "I always think of the day I stood before Miss Mackie at Hampton," he said.

He hired a pretty young teacher named Olivia Davidson. She became "lady principal." She worked as hard as Washington. Olivia, too, wanted to spend her life helping her people.

8. First Things First

An old plantation came up for sale. Washington borrowed some money from Hampton and bought it. The plantation had two cabins, a stable, and a hen-house. Washington and his students cleaned and painted. Then the school moved. The stable and hen-house became classrooms.

Meanwhile the lady principal was busy raising money to pay back the loan. The whole town helped. Some could give only a few pennies. Others came to work.

One day an old, old woman came. "I spent most of my life in slavery," she said. "I have saved six eggs. Please let these eggs help the new school."

"Thank you," Washington said. "No gift will ever mean more to me."

Washington told his students, "Bring your axes to school tomorrow. We will have our first chopping bee."

"We've never been to a chopping bee," students cried excitedly.

Washington led them into the woods. "Follow me," he said. He began chopping trees.

The students followed. Suddenly one cried, "Hey! This is nothing but cutting trees and clearing land."

"First things first," Washington explained. "First we will clear land. Then we will plant a farm so that we can eat."

Students grumbled, "We came here to school for book learning."

"Book learning? Why, of course!" Washington said. "But hand work and head work must go together. A good carpenter must know arithmetic. A good farmer must know science."

"But we want to be teachers," the students said.

"And you must teach Negroes that there is beauty and dignity in working with the hands." Washington said, "There is as much dignity in tilling a field as in writing a poem."

Summer came. Washington went to Malden to get married. His bride was his childhood sweetheart, Fannie Smith. She, too, had gone to Hampton. Fannie had beautiful eyes and a merry laugh.

"Next things next," Washington said. "We must have more buildings. Our students must live on the campus."

The first building was made of wood. "Our next will be of bricks," Washington told the students.

"Bricks?" students said. "There are no brickyards nearby."

"We will make our own bricks. There is good clay here."

"But have you ever made bricks, Mr. Washington?"

"We learn by doing."

Students dug the clay and shaped 25,000 bricks. It was a hard job. Washington made a special oven, or kiln, to bake them. But the kiln did not work right. The bricks crumbled. A second kiln failed. So did a third.

Washington sold his watch to get money for another kiln. Again bricks were shaped and baked. Everyone waited. When the kiln was opened, a shout went up. "Bricks! Perfect ones!"

Men from town came to buy bricks. They said, "We will help the school, because the school is helping the town."

"Yes," Washington said. "The town and school will each help the other."

That year a baby girl was born to Washington and Fannie. They named her Portia. A few months later Fannie died. Washington cared for baby Portia and worked harder than ever.

Then General Armstrong came to visit. The two men spent long hours talking and planning. "We must help the whole South," Armstrong said.

"Ah, yes," Washington promised. "I forgive the southern white man for keeping the Negroes as slaves. I will let no man drag me down so low as to make me hate him."

9. Mr. B.T.

The school grew rapidly. New buildings went up. More land was bought. New teachers came.

"Where will I get money for such a growing school?" Washington wondered.

General Armstrong gave the answer. He taught Washington how to make speeches to raise money.

Washington traveled all over the United States. He told people about the school. They sent money to Tuskegee. They sent clothes and blankets for the poor students.

By 1885 things brightened. John came. "Booker needs me," John said. He gave up his own work. He spent the rest of his life helping his brother to build Tuskegee. Later James, too, came to help.

And Washington married Olivia Davidson, the lady principal. Soon there were two little boys in the family, Booker Taliaferro, and Ernest Davidson.

One cold winter night their house caught on fire. The babies were saved. But Olivia caught a terrible cold and soon died.

"Mr. B.T." trained hands and minds at Tuskegee. At left, a machine shop class; below, a chemistry laboratory.

Washington was very sad, but he found comfort in his three children. He told them wonderful stories at bedtime. He took them for walks in the woods. They picked flowers and listened to bird songs. "Always stay close to nature," Washington taught.

When Washington went on trips, he bought gifts for John's children as well as for his own. Often he took one of the children with him. He took John's little girl all the way to California.

Small Portia loved music. How she loved to play the piano for her father! Washington was very proud of his little daughter.

Often, before Washington gave a speech, he recited it to Portia. "How do you like it?" he would ask.

"Oh, father, it's grand!" Portia would reply.

Washington was like a father to his students too. He knew each by name. They lovingly called him "Mr. B.T." Each year students went out to teach others what they had learned. Many opened schools of their own.

Washington told students, "We train your hand, head, and heart. And we help you in these ways that you, in turn, may help others."

He was too busy to take vacations. But he had his own garden. He raised chickens and pigs. He gathered eggs and vegetables for the family. "I rest when I am close to the soil," he said.

Washington loved horses. A rich white friend gave him a swift gray horse, Dexter. "No horse will ever run fast enough for you," the friend said. After a hard day's work Washington would mount Dexter and gallop over the countryside. Sometimes he would stop suddenly, very still, to hear a bird or a cricket singing.

Step by step, Washington made the school larger. The students who came often had no money. So they built the buildings themselves. They grew the food they ate. They made the things they needed. And they learned useful trades as they worked. "We are doing more than building a school," Washington said. "We are lifting a race."

A stranger came to visit Tuskegee. Later someone asked him, "Did you see Washington's school?"

"School!" the stranger cried. "I have seen Booker T. Washington's city."

10. A Famous Speech

It was September 1895. Atlanta, capital city of Georgia, buzzed with excitement. A big fair was about to open there. It would show the many uses of cotton. It would also show things the South had done since the Civil War.

Newspapers carried surprising news. Booker T. Washington would give one of the opening speeches.

A black man had never spoken at such an event in the South.

"What will he say?" people asked. "Will he say the South is unfair to Negroes? Will he spoil the fun of the fair?"

"What can I say?" Washington asked himself. "Negroes, northerners, and southerners, will all be listening. My own future, and that of my school and my race, will depend upon what I say."

Yes, visitors were there from every state and from other lands. Cannons boomed. Whistles tooted. Bands played. Parades marched.

The opening speeches began. The hall was packed. The governor, the mayor, and other famous people spoke.

Then Washington's turn came. He rose, holding a pencil in his hand. He stood tall and straight as an Indian chief. He turned his handsome head toward the sun. His voice rang out.

Washington begged all the people to work together to build up the South. He told blacks to stay in the South and to make friends with their white neighbors. He told them to get training, to do their work better, and to help the South grow.

He told white listeners to give black people a chance to learn. Blacks had been faithful workers. The two races could help each other, and the South.

Then Washington raised his hand. He told the people to obey the law and to work together. "This will bring into our beloved South a new heaven and a new earth."

White and black stood and cheered as one. Men tossed their hats into the air. Women waved their handkerchiefs. It was as though everyone had been put under a magic spell by the words of Booker T. Washington.

Newspapers said, "It was one of the greatest speeches ever given in the South."

And Washington became famous overnight. He was now a leader of the black race. Harvard University gave him an honorary degree. It was the first time a great American school had given a degree of honor to a black man. The president of Harvard said, "Booker Taliaferro Washington—teacher; wise helper of his race; good servant of God and country."

Washington gave other great speeches. Halls were packed wherever he spoke. He would speak to a group of college presidents and teachers. Then he would leave and talk to a group of poor blacks. He knew just what to say to every group. He loved to tell funny stories. He could make his listeners laugh one minute and cry the next.

In 1899, friends gave Washington money for a trip to Europe. He was now married to Margaret Murray, one of the teachers at Tuskegee. They were entertained by the most important people in Europe. They had tea with Queen Victoria in her castle. The boy born in a slave cabin was guest of the queen of England.

11. A New Day for Black People

The next year Washington wrote the story of his life. *Up from Slavery* became a best seller. The whole world read it. Later Washington wrote other books about his work and his race.

And like magic, he brought just the right teachers to work at the school. One teacher said, "It was teamwork that built Tuskegee."

The most famous teacher was George Washington Carver. He came to teach agricultural science. This gentle black scientist and Washington became close friends. Late at night the two walked peacefully over the campus. They planned help for the farmers.

"We'll show them how to make the soil richer," Carver said.

"And we'll teach them to keep pigs and cows," Washington added.

"They'll plant sweet potatoes, peanuts, and soybeans, along with cotton. Then the South will grow richer."

George Washington Carver in his laboratory. The great scientist found hundreds of new uses for peanuts, sweet potatoes, and cotton.

"And they'll have better schools," Washington said. "Then the South will grow wiser."

Carver's work brought worldwide fame to Tuskegee.

Washington's fame spread, too. He received more than 150 letters a day. Kings and statesmen asked his advice. President Theodore Roosevelt invited him to the White House for dinner. Dartmouth College gave him another degree of honor. Now he was called Dr. Washington.

Years passed. Soon it was 1906. "I can't believe that the school is 25 years old," Washington said. "And I am 50." What a grand celebration the school had that year!

In 1907 Portia married. Portia had studied music in Europe. She, too, helped Tuskegee. She trained the singers in the famous Tuskegee Choir.

Washington worked harder than ever. Sometimes he gave six speeches in a day. He often had to be away from Tuskegee. But daily letters told him just what was happening there. He even knew how many eggs the chickens laid, and what the students ate for dinner.

On his travels, Washington made friends with some of the richest men in America.

Julius Rosenwald was head of Sears, Roebuck and Company. Washington asked him, "Will you help the Negroes build schools?"

Rosenwald gave money for more than 5,000 black schools throughout the South.

Washington asked another friend, Miss Anna Jeanes, "Will you help us train teachers?"

Miss Jeanes gave a million dollars.

Andrew Carnegie, another famous American, helped. He said, "History is to know two Washingtons, one white, the other black, both fathers of their people."

Nineteen fifteen was a busy year. Washington became tired. He was asked to speak at a big meeting in the North. Before he left, he went to see Carver. The two men looked over the beautiful campus.

"Tuskegee has come a long way," Washington said.

The great educator on the speaker's platform and in his study. In later years Washington looked back on a life well spent in the service of his people and his country.

Carver smiled gently. "So have we. You and I were both born slaves. Yet, we are helping to build a great school."

"My school and my race," Washington said, "have both made progress. Now we look to the future. A new day for the Negroes lies ahead."

Washington went north. There, he became very sick. "Take me home," he said. "I was born in the South, I have lived and labored in the South, and I wish to die and be buried in the South."

He reached Tuskegee. Early the next morning he died peacefully. It was harvest time, his favorite season.

Washington gave many gifts to his country. Perhaps his greatest gift was the lesson he taught: All men are brothers.

Even today his name has magic. A southern farmer will say on a lovely morning, "It's going to be a wonderful day!"

"Ah, yes!" his wife will reply. "It's going to be a real Booker T. Washington day."

Index

166

Folger, Ben, 28, 29
Freedmen's Hospital, 48, 51
Freedmen's Village, 43, 44 (pic), 46, 47
Freed slaves (freedmen), 87
    aid to, 48, 52, 53, 55, 130, 144, 151
    discrimination against, 48, 127, 128
    education of, 44, 45, 145, 151
    living conditions of, 41, 44, 51, 138, 150
Fugitive Slave Law, 115

G

Garfield, James A., 88
Garrison, William Lloyd, 74, 75, 76
Gilbert, Olive, 33, 35

H

Hampton Institute, 142, 143, 145, 146, 149
Harpers Ferry, 84, 123–124
Harriet Tubman Home, 131
Harriet Tubman: The Moses of Her People, 130

I

Isabella (Belle). *See* Truth, Sojourner

J

Johnson, Andrew, 47, 48
Johnson, Nathan, 74

L

Liberator, 74
Lincoln, Abraham, 40, 41, 42, 43, 47, 84, 85, 87, 125, 135
Lord, Nathalie, 145

M

Mackie, Mary, 144, 151
Murray, Anna. *See* Douglass, Anna
Murray, Margaret. *See* Washington, Margaret

N

Narrative of the Life of Frederick Douglass, an American Slave, 78
Neely, John, 13, 14
North Star, The, 79, 80, 91

P

Philadelphia Vigilance Committee, 114
Pierson, Elijah, 27, 28, 29
Pitts, Helen. *See* Douglass, Helen
Post, Amy, 34–35

Q

Quakers, 21, 23, 113

R

Rosenwald, Julius, 163
Ross, Benjamin (father of Harriet Tubman), 96, 101, 107, 110
Ruggles, David, 72

S

Schryver, Martin, 15, 16
Slaves,
    auctions of, 12, 13 (pic), 61
    emancipation of, 20, 40, 85, 86
    living conditions of, 10, 19, 62 (pic), 63, 96–97, 134, 135
    treatment of, 15, 17, 61, 66–67, 98
    uprisings of, 104, 123
Smith, Fannie. *See* Washington, Fannie
Stanton, Elizabeth Cody, 80
Still, William, 114, 115
Stowe, Harriet Beecher, 38

T

Tilton, Theodore, 91
Truth, Sojourner (Belle), 9 (pic), 54 (pic)
    and antislavery movement, 33, 34, 35, 36, 37, 39, 40